Mary Platt Parmele

The Story of Spain

Briefly Told

Mary Platt Parmele

The Story of Spain
Briefly Told

ISBN/EAN: 9783337240059

Printed in Europe, USA, Canada, Australia, Japan

Cover: Foto ©ninafisch / pixelio.de

More available books at **www.hansebooks.com**

RT HISTORY OF SPAIN.

THE STORY OF
SPAIN
BRIEFLY TOLD

BY

MARY PLATT PARMELE

AUTHOR OF "FRANCE," "ENGLAND," "UNITED STATES,"
"GERMANY," "WHO, WHEN, AND WHAT?" ETC.

PUBLISHED FOR THE

BAY VIEW READING CIRCLE

CENTRAL OFFICE, FLINT, MICH.

1898

PRESS OF THE
CONTINENTAL PUBLISHING CO.,
25 Park Place, New York.

PREFACE.

IN presenting this book to the public the author can only reiterate what she has already said in works of a similar kind: that she has tried to exclude the mass of confusing details which often make the reading of history a dreary task; and to keep closely to those facts which are vital to the unfolding of the narrative. This is done under a strong conviction that the essential facts in history are those which reveal and explain the development of a nation, rather than the incidents, more or less entertaining, which have attended such development. And also under another conviction: that a little, thoroughly comprehended, is better than much imperfectly remembered and understood.

M. P. P.

NEW YORK. *June* 15, 1898.

CONTENTS.

CHAPTER I.
            PAGE
Ancient Iberia—The Basques—The Keltiberians—The Phenicians—Cadiz Founded, . . . 1

CHAPTER II.
Struggle between Phenicians and Assyrians—Founding of Carthage—Decline of Phenicia—Rise of Roman Power—First Punic War, . 9

CHAPTER III.
Hamilcar—Hannibal—Siege and Fall of Saguntum—Rome Invades Spain—Scipio's Policy—Cadiz, (Gades) Surrendered to the Romans—By What Steps IBERIA Became SPAIN—Fall of Carthaginian Power—How Spain Became a Roman Province, ... 15

CHAPTER IV.
Sertorius—Story of the White Hind—Rome Fights Her Own Battles on Spanish Soil—Battle of Munda—Cæsar Declared Dictator—The Ides of March—Octavius Augustus—Spain Latinized—Four Hundred Years of Peace, ... 24

CHAPTER V.

Northern Races in the History of Civilization—Roman Empire Expiring—Ataulfus—Attila and the Huns—Theodoric—Evaric Completes Conquest of Spanish Peninsula—Europe Teutonized—Difference between Anglo-Saxon and Latin Races, ... 30

CHAPTER VI.

Ulfilas—Arianism—The Spanish Language—Brunhilde—Leovigild—His Son's Apostasy—Arianism Ceases to be the Established Religion of Spain, ... 39

CHAPTER VII.

Toledo—Church of Santa Maria—Wamba, . . 45

CHAPTER VIII.

Decline of Visigoths—Roderick—Count Julian's Treachery—Mahommedanism—Tarif — Prophecy Found in the Enchanted Tower—Tarik—Roderick's Defeat and Death—Moslem Empire Established in Spain, ... 50

CHAPTER IX.

Musa's Dream of European Conquest—Charles Martel—Characteristics of Mahommedan Rule—Mission of the Saracen in Europe—The Germ of a Christian Kingdom in the North of Spain, ... 58

CHAPTER X.

Pelayo and the Cave of Covadonga—Alfonso I.—Berbers and Arabs at War on African Coast—War Extends to Spain—The Omeyyad Khalifs Superseded by the Abbasides—Abd-er-Rahman—Omeyyad Dynasty Established at Cordova—Ineffectual Attempt of the Abbasides to Overthrow Abd-er-Rahman—Character of This Conqueror, ... 64

CHAPTER XI.

Charlemagne—Battle of Roncesvalles, . . . 69

CHAPTER XII.

Conditions after Death of Abd-er-Rahman—Abd-er-Rahman II.—Arab Refinements—Eulogius and the Christian Martyrs—Abd-er-Rahman III.—A Khalifate—At Cordova—The Great Mosque—The City of "The Fairest"—Death of Abd-er-Rahman III., ... 72

CHAPTER XIII.

Rough Cradle of a Spanish Nationality in the Asturias—Alfonso III. and His Hidalgos and Dons—Guerrilla Warfare with Moors—Jealousies and Strife between Christian Kingdoms—Civil War—Almanzor—Ruin of Christian State Seemed Imminent—Death of Almanzor—Berber Revolt—Anarchy in Moorish State—A Khalif Begging a Crust of Bread—Berbers Destroy Cordova—Library Burned—City of The Fairest a Ruin—Asturias—Leon and Castile United—Alfonso VI.—The Cid—Triumph of Christians—

Moors Ask Aid of the Almoravides—Christians Driven Back—Death of the Cid—A Dynasty of the Almoravides—The Alhomades—The Great Mahdi—Moorish People Become Subject to Emperor of Morocco—His Designs upon Europe—The Pope Proclaims a Crusade—Alhomades Driven out of Spain by Christians—Moorish Kingdom Reduced to Province of Granada, ... 78

CHAPTER XIV.

European Conditions in Thirteenth Century—Visigoth Kings Recover Their Land — Its Changed Conditions—Effect of Arab Civilization upon Spanish Nation—Fernando III.—Spain Draws into Closer Companionship with European States—Alfonso X.—Spain Becoming Picturesque—The Bull-Fight—Beautiful Granada—The Alhambra, ... 87

CHAPTER XV.

Perpetual Civil War between Spanish States—Castile and Aragon Absorb the Others and in Conflict for Supremacy — Pedro the Cruel—The Black Prince His Champion against Aragon—John of Gaunt—His Claim upon the Throne of Castile—His Final Compromise—Political Conditions Contrasted with Those of Other States, ... 94

CHAPTER XVI.

Death of Juan II.—Enrique IV.—Isabella—Her Marriage with Ferdinand of Aragon—Isabella

Crowned Queen of Castile—Ferdinand, King of Aragon—The Two Crowns United—Characteristics of the Two Sovereigns—The Inquisition Created—Jews Driven out of the Kingdom—Abdul-Hassan's Defiance—Zahara — Family Troubles at the Alhambra—Ayesha and Boabdil—Alhama Captured by Ferdinand—Boabdil Supplants His Father—Massacre of the Abencerrages—Granada Besieged—Its Capitulation—Moorish Rule Ended in Spain, . . . 100

CHAPTER XVII.

Columbus and Isabella—Isabella's Private Griefs—Her Death—Charles, King under a Regency—Charles Elected Emperor of Germany—Spain during His Reign—Cruelties in the East and in the West—Vain Struggle with Protestantism—Abdication and Death of Charles, . . . 108

CHAPTER XVIII.

Philip II.—Union of Spain and Portugal—The Duke of Alva in the Netherlands—War with England—Spanish Armada Destroyed—Death of Philip II.—Spain's Decline—Glory of the Name Castilian, ... 117

CHAPTER XIX.

Philip III.—Rebellion of the Moriscos—Last of the Moors Conveyed to African Coast—Don Quixote—Philip IV.—Louis XIV. Marries Spanish Infanta—A Diminishing Kingdom—Carlos II.—First Collision between Anglo-Saxon and Spaniard in America—Close of Hapsburg Dynasty in Spain, ... 125

CHAPTER XX.

PAGE

New European Conditions—Louis XIV.—War of the "Spanish Succession"—Marlborough Checks Louis at Blenheim—Archduke Abandons Sovereignty in Spain—Peace of Utrecht —Further Dismemberment of Spain—Gibraltar Passes to England—Bourbon Dynasty—Commences with Philip V.—Ferdinand VI.—Carlos III.—Expulsion of the Jesuits, ... 131

CHAPTER XXI.

A Dismantled Kingdom—Spanish-American Colonies—England and France at War over American Boundaries—Spain the Ally of France— Loss of Some of Her West India Islands, and Capture of Havana and Manila by British— Florida Given in Exchange for Return of Conquered Territory—Growing Irritiation against England—France Aids American Colonies in War with England—Spain's Satisfaction at Their Success—Its Effect in Peru—Revolution in France—Rapid Rise of Napoleon—Carlos IV. Removed and Joseph Bonaparte King—Spain Joins Napoleon in War against England—Trafalgar—Arthur Wellesley—Joseph Flees from His Kingdom, ... 137

CHAPTER XXII.

Liberal Sentiment Developing — Constitution of 1812—Ferdinand VI. and Reactionary Measures — Revolt of all the Spanish-American Colonies — The Holy Alliance—The Monroe Doctrine—Revolution in Spain—Spain under

CONTENTS. xiii

the Protectorate of the Holy Alliance—Ferdinand Reinstated—Two Political Parties—Six Spanish-American Colonies Freed, . . . 144

CHAPTER XXIII.

The Salic Law and the Princess Isabella—The Carlists—Regency of Christine—Isabella II.—Her Expulsion from Spain—Amadeo—An Era of Republicanism—Castelar—Alfonso XII. Recalled—His Brief Reign and Death—Alfonso XIII., ... 150

CHAPTER XXIV.

Birth of an Insurgent Party in Cuba—Ten Years' War—Impossible Reforms Promised—Revolution Started by José Marti, 1895—Attitude of the American Government—General Weyler's Methods—Effect upon Sentiment in America—Destruction of the Battle-Ship *Maine*—Verdict of Court of Inquiry—War Declared between Spain and America—The Approaching End, . 154

A SHORT HISTORY OF SPAIN.

CHAPTER I.

No name is more fraught with picturesque and romantic interest than that of the " Spanish Peninsula."

After finishing this rare bit of handiwork nature seems to have thrown up a great ragged wall, stretching from sea to sea, to protect it; and the Pyrenees have stood for ages a frowning barrier, descending toward France on the northern side from gradually decreasing heights—but on the Spanish side in wild disorder, plunging down through steep chasms, ravines, and precipices—with sharp cliffs towering thousands of feet skyward, which better than standing armies protect the sunny plains below.

But the " Spanish Peninsula," at the time we are about to consider, was neither " spanish " nor was it a peninsula. At the dawn of history this sunny corner of Europe was known as *Iberia*, and its people as *Iberians*.

Time has effaced all positive knowledge of this aboriginal race; but they are believed to have come from the south, and to have been allied to the Libyans, who inhabited the northern coast of Africa. In fact, *Iberi* in the Libyan tongue meant *freeman;* and *Berber*, which was the plural form of that word, was the term by which all of these western peoples were known to the Ancient Egyptians.

But it is suspected that the Iberians found it an easy matter to flow into the land south of the Pyrenees, and that they needed no boats for the transit. There has always existed a tradition of the joining of the two continents, and now it is believed by geologists that an isthmus once really stretched across to the African coast at the narrowest point of the Straits, at a time when the waters of a Mediterranean gulf, and the waters flowing over the sands of Sahara, together found their outlet in the Indian Ocean.

There is also a tradition that the adventurous Phenicians, who are known to have been in Iberia as early as 1300 B. C., cut a canal through the narrow strip of land, and then built a bridge across the canal. But a bridge was a frail link by which to hold the mighty continents together. The Atlantic, glad of such an entrance to the great gulf beyond, must have rushed impetuously through, gradually widening the opening, and thus, at last, permanently severed Europe and Africa; drained the Sahara dry; transformed the Mediterranean gulf into a Mediterranean Sea; and created a " Spanish Peninsula."

How long this fair Peninsula was the undisturbed home of the Iberians no one knows. Behind the rocky ramparts of the Pyrenees they may have remained for centuries unconscious of the Aryan torrent which was flooding Western Europe as far as the British Isles. Nothing has been discovered by which we may reconstruct this prehistoric people and (perhaps) civilization. But their physical characteristics we are enabled to guess; for just as we find in Cornwall, England, lingering traces of the ancient Britons, so in the mountain fastnesses of northern Spain linger the *Basques*, who are by many supposed to be the last survivors of that mysterious primitive race.

The language of the Basques bears no resemblance to any of the Indo-European, nor indeed to any known tongue. It is so difficult, so intricate in construction, that only those who learn it in infancy can ever master it. It is said that, in Basque, "you spell Solomon, and pronounce it Nebuchadnezzar." Its antiquity is so great that one legend calls it the "language of the angels," and another says that *Tubal* brought it to Spain before the lingual disaster at Babel! And still another relates that the devil once tried to learn it, but that, after studying it for seven years and learning only three words, he gave it up in despair.

A language which, without literature, can so resist change, can so persist unmodified by another tongue spoken all around and about it, must have great antiquity; and there is every reason to believe that the Basque is a survival of the tongue spoken by the primitive Iberians, before the Kelts began to flow over and around the Pyrennees; and also that the physical characteristics of this people are the same as those of their ancient progenitors; small-framed, dark, with a faint suggestion of the Semitic in their swarthy faces.

We cannot say when it occurred, but at last the powerful, fair-haired Kelts had surmounted the barrier and were mingled with this non-Aryan people, and the resulting race thus formed was known to antiquity as the *Keltiberians*.

It is probable that the rugged Kelt easily absorbed the race of more delicate type, and made it, in religion and customs, not unlike the Keltic Aryan in Gaul. But the physical characteristics of the other and primitive race are indelibly stamped upon the Spanish people; and it is probably to the Iberian strain in the blood that may be traced the small, dark type of men which largely prevails in Spain, and to some extent also in central and southern France.

But the Keltiberians were Keltic in their religion. There are now in Spain the usual monuments found wherever Druid worship prevailed. Huge blocks of stone, especially in Cantabria and Lusitania (Portugal), standing alone or in circles, tell the story of Druidical rites, and of the worship of the ocean, the wind, and the thunder, and of the placating of the powers of nature by human sacrifices.

The mingling of the Kelts and the Iberians

in varying proportions in different parts of Spain, and in some places (as among the Basques) their mingling not at all, produced that diversity of traits which distinguished the *Asturians* in the mountain gorges from their neighbors the *Cantabrians*, and both these from the *Catalonians* in the northeast and the *Gallicians* on the northwest coast, and from the *Lusitanians*, where now is Portugal; and still more distinguished the *Basques*, in the rocky ravines of the Pyrenees, from each and all of the others. And yet these unlike members of one family were collectively known as Keltiberians.

While this race—hardy, temperate, brave, and superstitious—was leading its primitive life upon the Iberian peninsula, while they were shooting arrows at the sky to threaten the thunder, drawing their swords against the rising tide, and prizing iron more dearly than their abundant gold and silver, because they could hammer it into hooks, and swords, and spears—there had long existed in the East a group of wonderful civilizations: the Egyptian, hoary with age and steeped in wisdom and in wickedness; the *Chaldeans*, who, with " looks commercing with the skies," were the fathers of astronomy; the *Assyrians* and *Babylonians*, with their wonderful cities of *Nineveh* and *Babylon*, and the Phenicians, with their no less famous cities of *Sidon* and *Tyre*. Sidon, which was the more ancient of these two, is said to have been founded by Sidon, the son of Canaan, who was the great-grandson of Noah.

Of all these nations it was the Phenicians who were the most adventurous. They were a Semitic people, Syrian in blood, and their home was a narrow strip of coast on the east of the Mediterranean, where a group of free cities was joined into a confederacy held together by a strong national spirit.

Of these cities Sidon was once the head, but in time Tyre eclipsed it in splendor, and writers, sacred and profane, have sung her glories.

These Phenicians had a genius for commerce and trade. They scented a bargain from afar, and knew how to exchange " their broidered work, and fine linen, and coral, and agate " (1 Kings xxvii. 16), their glassware and their wonderful cloths dyed in Tyrian scarlet and purple, for the spices and jewels of the East, and for the gold and silver and the ivory and the ebony of the south and west.

Their ships were coursing the Red Sea and the Persian Gulf and bringing back treasures from India and searching every inlet in the Mediterranean, and finally, either through the canal they had cut, or the straits it had made, they sailed as far as the British Isles and brought back tin.

But the gold and silver of the Iberian Peninsula were more alluring than the spices of India or the tin of Britain. So upon the Spanish coast they made permanent settlements and built cities. As early as 1100 B. C. they had founded beyond the " Pillars of Hercules," the City of *Gades* (Cadiz), a walled and fortified town, and had taught the Kelt-iberians how to open and work their gold and silver mines systematically; and in exchange they brought an old civilization, with new luxuries, new ideas and customs into the lives of the simple people.

But they bestowed something far beyond this—something more enriching than silver and gold,—an alphabet,—and it is to the Phenicians that we are indebted for the alphabet now in use throughout the civilized world.

CHAPTER II.

SUCH an extension of power, and the acquisition of sources of wealth so boundless, excited the envy of other nations.

The Greeks are said to have been in the Iberian peninsula long before the fall of Troy, where they came with a fleet from Zante, in the Ionian Sea, and in memory of that place, called the city they founded Zacynthus, which name in time became *Saguntum*. Now they sent more expeditions and founded more cities on the Spanish coast; and the Babylonians, and the Assyrians, and, at a later time, the Persians and the Greeks, all took up arms against these insatiate traders.

Phenician supremacy was not easily maintained with so many jealous rivals in the field, and it was rudely shaken in 850 B. C., when

"The Assyrians came down like a wolf on the fold,
Their cohorts all gleaming with purple and gold,

and the Phenician power was partially broken at its source in the East.

It is with thrilling interest that we read

Isaiah's prophecy of the destruction of Tyre, which was written at this very time. For the Phenicians were the *Canaanites* of Bible history, and " Hiram King of Tyre " was their king; and his " navy," which, together with Solomon's " came once in three years from *Tarshish*," was their navy; and *Tarshish* was none other than *Tartessus*, their own province, just beyond Gibraltar on the Spanish coast. Nor is it at all improbable that Spanish gold was used to adorn the temple which the great Solomon was building. (1 Kings ix., x.) Shakspere, who says all things better than anyone else, makes Othello find in the fatal handkerchief " confirmation strong as proofs from holy writ." Where can be found " confirmation " stronger than these " proofs from holy writ "? And where a more magnificent picture of the luxury, the sumptuous Oriental splendor of this nation at that period, than in Ezekiel, chapters xxvii., xxviii.? What an eloquent apostrophe to Tyre— " thou that art situate at the entry of the sea, a merchant of the people, for *many isles*."— " With thy wisdom and with thine understanding thou hast gotten thee riches," and, " by thy great wisdom and by thy *traffick* hast thou increased, and thine heart is lifted up." And then follows the terrible arraignment—" because of the iniquity of thy *traffick*." And then the final prediction of ruin—" I will bring thee to ashes upon the earth "; " thou shalt be a terror, and *never* shalt thou be any more." Where in any literature can we find such lurid splendor of description, and such a powerful appeal to the imagination of the reader! And where could the student of history find a more graphic and accurate picture of a vanished civilization!

In 850 B. C., the same year in which the Assyrians partly subjugated the Phenicians in the East, the city of Carthage was founded upon the north coast of Africa, and there commenced a movement, with that city as its center, which drew together all their scattered possessions into a Punic confederacy. This was composed of the islands of Sardinia, Corsica, part of Sicily, the Balearic Isles, and the cities and colonies upon the Spanish Peninsula and African coast. As the power of this confederacy expands, the name Phenician passes away and that of *Carthaginian* takes its place in history.

Carthage became a mighty city, and controlled with a strong hand the scattered empire which had been planted by the Syrian tradesmen. Carthaginian merchants and miners were in Tartessus, and were planting cities and colonies throughout the peninsula, and a torrent of Carthaginian life was thus pouring into Spain for many hundred years, and the blood of the two races must have freely mingled.

There are memorials of this time now existing, not only in Phenician coins, medals, and ruins, but in the names of the cities. *Barcelona*, named after the powerful family of Barca in Carthage, to which Hannibal belonged. *Carthagena*, a memorial of Carthage, which meant "the city"; and even *Cordova* is traced to its primitive form,—Kartah-duba,—meaning "an important city." While *Isabella*, the name most famous in Spanish annals, has a still greater antiquity; and was none other than Jezebel—after the beautiful daughter of the King of Sidon (the "*Zidoneans*"), who married Ahab, and lured him to his downfall. And we are told that this wicked siren whose dreadful fate Elijah foretold, was cousin to Dido, she who Virgil tells us "wept in silence" for the faithless Æneas.

With what a strange thrill do we find these threads of association between history sacred and profane, and both mingled with the modern history of Spain.

But Phenicia, for the "iniquity of her traffick," was doomed. The roots of this old Asiatic tree had been slowly and surely perishing, while her branches in the West were expanding. In the year 332 B. C. the siege and destruction of Tyre, predicted five hundred years before by Isaiah, was accomplished by Alexander the Great, and the words of the prophet found their complete fulfillment,— that the people of Tarshish should find no city, no port, no welcome, when they came back to Syria!

But on the northern coast of the Mediterranean there was another power which was waxing, while the Carthaginian was waning. The chief occupation of the Roman Republic was not trade, but conquest. A bitter enmity existed between the two nations, and Rome was determined to break this grasping Asiatic confederacy and to drive it out of Europe. The Spanish Peninsula they knew little about, but the rich islands near her own coast—they must be hers.

When, after the first Punic war (264-241 B. C.), the Carthaginians saw Sardinia and Sicily torn from them, Hamilcar, their great general, determined upon a plan of vengeance which should make of Italy a Punic province. His people were strong upon the sea, but for this war of invasion they must have an army, too. So he conceived the idea of making Spain the basis of his military operations, and recruiting an immense army from the Iberian Peninsula.

CHAPTER III.

THE Carthaginian occupation of Spain had not extended much beyond the coast, and had been rather in the nature of a commercial alliance with the Spaniards. Now Hamilcar determined by placating, and by bribes, and by force if necessary, to take possession of the Peninsula for his own purposes, and to make of the people a Punic nation under the complete dominion of Carthage. So his first task was to win, or to subdue, the Keltiberians. He built the city of New Carthage (now Carthagena), he showed the people how to develop their immense resources, and by promises of increased prosperity won the confidence and sympathy of the nation, and soon had a population of millions from which to recruit its army.

When his son Hannibal was nine years old, at his father's bidding he placed his hand upon the altar and swore eternal enmity to Rome. The fidelity of the boy to his oath made a great deal of history. He took up the task when his father laid it down, inaugurated the second Punic war (218-201 B. C.); and for forty years carried on one of the most determined and desperate struggles the world has ever seen.

Saguntum was an old city in Valencia which was said to have been founded by the ancient Greeks before Homer sang of Troy, or, indeed, before Helen brought ruin upon that city. At all events its antiquity was greater even than that of the Phenician cities in Spain, and after being long forgotten by the Greeks it had drifted under Roman protection. It was the only spot in Spain which acknowledged allegiance to Rome; and for that reason was marked for destruction as an act of defiance.

The Saguntines sent an embassy to Rome. These men made a pitiful and passionate appeal in the Senate Chamber: " Romans, allies, friends! help! help! Hannibal is at the gates of our city. Hannibal, the sworn enemy of Rome. Hannibal the terrible. Hannibal who fears not the gods, neither keeps faith with men. [" Punic faith " was a byword.] O Romans, fathers, friends! help while there is yet time."

But they found they had a "protector" who did not protect. The senators sent an embassy to treat with Hannibal, but no soldiers. So, with desperate courage, the Saguntines defended their beleaguered city for weeks, hurling javelins, thrusting their lances, and beating down the besiegers from the walls. They had no repeating rifles nor dynamite guns, but they had the terrible *falaric*, a shaft of fir with an iron head a yard long, at the point of which was a mass of burning tow, which had been dipped in pitch. When a breach was made in the walls, the inflowing army would be met by a rain of this deadly falaric, which was hurled with telling power and precision. Then, in the short interval of rest this gave them, men, women, and children swiftly repaired the broken walls before the next assault.

But at last the resourceful Hannibal abandoned his battering rams, and with pickaxes undermined the wall, which fell with a crash. When asked to surrender, the chief men of the city kindled a great fire in the market-place, into which they then threw all the silver and gold in the treasury, their own gold and silver and garments and furniture, and then cast themselves headlong into the flames. This was their answer.

Saguntum, which for more than a thousand years had looked from its elevation out upon the sea, was no more, and its destruction was one of the thrilling tragedies of ancient history. On its site there exists to-day a town called *Mur Viedro* (old walls), and these old walls are the last vestige of ancient Saguntum.

In order to understand the indifference of Rome to the Spanish Peninsula at this time, it must be remembered that Spain was then the uttermost verge of the known world, beyond which was only a dread waste of waters and of mystery. To the people of Tyre and of Greece, the "Pillars of Hercules" had marked the limit beyond which there was nothing; and those two columns, Gibraltar and Ceuta, with the legend *ne plus ultra* entwined about them, still survive, as a symbol, in the arms of Spain and upon the Spanish coins; and what is still more interesting to Americans, in the familiar mark ($) which represents a dollar. (The English name for the Spanish *peso* is *pillar-dollar*.)

Now Rome was aroused from its apathy.

It sent an army into Spain, led by Scipio the Elder, known as Scipio Africanus. When he fell, his son, only twenty-four years old, stood up in the Roman Forum and offered to fill the undesired post; and, in 210 B.C., Scipio "the Younger"—and the greater—took the command—as Livy eloquently says—"between the tombs of his father and his uncle," who had both perished in Spain within a month.

The chief feature of Scipio's policy was, while he was defeating Hannibal in battles, to be undermining him with his native allies; and to make that people realize to what hard taskmasters they had bound themselves; and by his own manliness and courtesy and justice to win them to his side.

He marched his army swiftly and unexpectedly upon New Carthage, the capital and center of the whole Carthaginian movement, sent his fleet to blockade the city, and planned his moves with such precision that the fleet for the blockade and the army for the siege arrived before the city on the same day.

Taken entirely by surprise, New Carthage was captured without a siege. Not one of the inhabitants was spared, and spoil of fabulous amounts fell to the victors.

It seems like a fairy tale—or like the story of Mexico and Peru 1800 years later—to read of 276 golden bowls which were brought to Scipio's tent, countless vessels of silver, and 18 tons of coined and wrought silver.

But the richest part of the prize was the 750 Spanish hostages—high in rank of course—whom the various tribes had given in pledge of their fidelity to Carthage. Now Scipio held these pledges, and they were a menace and a promise. They were Roman slaves, but he could by kindness, and by holding out the hope of emancipation, placate and further bind to him the native people.

By an exercise of tact and clemency Scipio gained such an ascendancy over the inhabitants, and so moved were they by this unexpected generosity and kindness, that many would gladly have made him their king.

But he seems to have been the "noblest Roman of them all," and when saluted as king on one occasion he said: " Never call me king. Other nations may revere that name, but no Roman can endure it. My soldiers have given me a more honorable title—that of general."

Such nobility, such a display of Roman virtue, was a revelation to these barbarians; and they felt the grandeur of the words, though they could not quite understand them. They were won to the cause of Rome, and formed loyal alliances with Scipio which they never broke.

In the year 206 B. C. Gades (Cadiz), the last stronghold, was surrendered to the Romans, and the entire Spánish Peninsula had been wrenched from the Carthaginians.

Iberia was changed to *Hispania*, and fifteen years later (197 B. C.) the whole of the Peninsula was organized into a Roman province, thenceforth known, not as *Iberia*, nor yet *Hispania;* but *Spain*, and its people as *Spaniards*.

At the end of the third Punic war (149-146 B. C.), the ruin of the Carthaginians was complete. Hannibal had died a fugitive and a suicide. His nation had not a single ship upon the seas, nor a foot of territory upon the earth, and the great city of Carthage was plowed and sowed with salt. History had made her last record in the life of an ancient people— "*Carthago est delenda.*"

It was really only a limited portion of the Peninsula; a fringe of provinces upon the south and east coast, which had been under Carthaginian and now acknowledged Roman dominion. Beyond these the Keltiberian tribes in the center formed a sort of confederation, and consented to certain alliances with the Romans; while beyond them, intrenched in their own impregnable mountain fastnesses, were brave, warlike, independent tribes, which had never known anything but freedom, whose names even Rome had not yet heard. The stern virtue and nobility of Scipio proved a delusive promise. Rome had not an easy task, and other and brutal methods were to be employed in subduing stubborn tribes and making of the whole a Latin nation. In one of the defiles of the Pyrenees there may now be seen the ruins of fortifications built by Cato the Elder, not long after Scipio, which show how early those free people in the north were made to feel the iron heel of the master and to learn their lesson of submission.

The century which followed Scipio's conquest was one of dire experience for Spain. A Roman army was trampling out every vestige of freedom in provinces which had known nothing else; and more than that, Roman diplomacy was making of their new possession a fighting ground for the civil war which was then raging at Rome; and partisans of Marius and of Sylla were using and slaughtering the native tribes in their own desperate struggle. Roman rule was arrogant and oppressive, Roman governors cruel, arbitrary, and rapacious, and the boasted " Roman virtue " seemed to have been left in Rome, when treaties were made only to be violated at pleasure.

CHAPTER IV.

As nature delights in adorning the crevices of crumbling ruins with mosses and graceful lichens, so literature has busied itself with these historic ruins; and Cervantes has made the siege of Numantia (134 B. C.)—more terrible even than that of Saguntum—the subject of a poem, in which he depicts the horrors of the famine.

Lira, the heroine, answers her ardent lover Mirando in high-flown Spanish phrase, which, when summed up in plain English prose, means that she cannot listen to his wooing, because she is so hungry—which, in view of the fact that she has not tasted food for weeks, seems to us not surprising!

Sertorius, whose story is told by Plutarch, affords another picturesque subject for Corneille in one of his most famous tragedies. This Roman was an adherent of Marius in the long struggle with Sylla, and while upholding his cause in Spain he won to his side the people of Lusitania (Portugal), who made him their ruler, and helped him to fight the great army of the opposing Roman faction, part of which was led by Pompey.

Mithridates, in Asia Minor, was also in conflict with Sylla, and sent an embassy to Sertorius which led to a league between the two for mutual aid, and for the defense of the cause of Marius. But senators of his own party became jealous of the great elevation of Sertorius, and conspired to assassinate him at a feast to which he was invited. So ended (72 B. C.) one of the most picturesque characters and interesting episodes in the difficult march of barbarous Spain toward enlightenment and civilization.

Sertorius seems to have been a great administrator as well as fighter, and must also be counted one of the civilizers of Spain. He founded a school at Osca,—now Huesca,—where he had Roman and Greek masters for the Spanish youth. And it is interesting to learn that there is to-day at that city a university which bears the title "University of Sertorius."

But it is not the valor nor the sagacity of Sertorius which made him the favorite of poets; but the story of the White Hind, which he made to serve him so ingeniously in establishing his authority with the Lusitanians.

A milk-white fawn, on account of its rarity, was given him by a peasant. He tamed her, and she became his constant companion, unaffrighted even in the tumult of battle. He saw that the people began to invest the little animal with supernatural qualities; so, finally, he confided to them that she was sent to him by the Goddess Diana, who spoke to him through her, and revealed important secrets.

Such is the story which Corneille and writers in other lands have found so fascinating, and which an English author has made the subject of his poem " The White Hind of Sertorius."

Another Roman civil war, more pregnant of great results, was to be fought out in Spain. Julius Cæsar's conspiracy against the Roman Republic, and his desperate fight with Pompey for the dictatorship, long drenched Spanish soil with blood, and had its final culmination (after Pompey's tragic death in Egypt) in Cæsar's victory over Pompey's sons at Munda, in Spain, 45 B. C.

With this event, the military triumphs and

the intrigues of Cæsar had accomplished his purpose. He was declared *Imperator*, perpetual Dictator of Rome, and religious sacrifices were decreed to him as if he were a god. Unconscious of the chasm which was yawning at his feet he haughtily accepted the honors and adulation of men who were at that very moment conspiring for his death. On the fatal "Ides of March" (44 B. C.) he was stricken in the Senate Chamber by the hands of his friends, and the great Cæsar lay dead at the feet of Pompey's statue.

The world had reached a supreme crisis in its existence. Two events—the most momentous it has ever known—were at hand: the birth of a Roman Empire, which was to perish in a few centuries, after a life of amazing splendor; and the birth of a spiritual kingdom, which would never die!

Cæsar's nephew, Octavius Augustus, by gradual approaches reached the goal toward which no doubt his greater uncle was moving. After defeating Brutus and Cassius at Philippi (42 B. C.) and then after destroying his only competitor, Antony, at Actium (31 B. C.) he assumed the imperial purple under the name of Augustus. The title sounded harmless, but its wearer had founded the "Roman Empire."

At last there was peace. Spain was pacified, and only here and there did she struggle in the grasp of the Romans. Augustus, to make sure of the permanence of this pacification, himself went to the Peninsula. He built cities in the plains, where he compelled the stubborn mountaineers to reside, and established military colonies in the places they had occupied.

Saragossa was one of these cities in the plains, and its name was "Cæsar Augusta," and many others have wandered quite as far from their original names, which may, however, still be traced.

It is said that "the annals of the happy are brief." Let us hope that poor Spain, so long harried by fate, was happy in the next four hundred years, for her story can be briefly told. She seemed to have settled into a state of eternal peace. It was a period not of external events, but of a process—an internal process of assimilation. Spain, in every department of its life, was becoming Latinized.

A people of rare intellectual activity had been united to the life of Rome at the moment of her greatest intellectual elevation. Was it strange that no Roman province ever produced so long a list of historians, poets, philosophers, as did Southern Spain after the Augustan conquest? When we read the list of great Roman authors who were born in Spain—the three Senecas, one of whom, the author and wit, opened his veins at the command of Nero (65 A. D.), and another, the Gallio of the book of Acts; also Lucan, Martial, and Quintilian, when we read these names native to Spain, it seems as if the source of inspiration had removed from the banks of the Tiber to the banks of the Guadalquivir.

Nowhere can the student of Roman antiquities find a richer field than in Spain. And not only that, there is to-day in the manners and customs, and in the habits of the peasantry, a pervading atmosphere of the classic land which adopted them, which all that has occurred since has been powerless to efface, while the language of Spain is Latin to its core. Nor is this strange when we reflect that they were under this powerful influence for a period as long as from Christopher Columbus to the Spanish-American War!

CHAPTER V.

IN the history of nations there is one fact which again and again with startling uniformity repeats itself. The rough, strong races from the north menace, and at last rudely dominate more highly civilized but less hardy races at the South, to the ultimate benefit of both, although with much present discomfort to the conquered race!

In Greece it was first the rude Hellenes who overran the Pelasgians. And again, long after that, there was another descent of fierce northern barbarians,—the Dorians from Epirus,—who, when they took possession of the Peloponnesus and became the *Spartans*, infused that vigorous strain without which the history of Greece might have been a very tame affair. In the British Isles it was the Picts and Scots, who would have done the same thing with England, perhaps, if the Angles and Saxons had not come to the rescue, while Spain had her own Picts and Scots in the mountain tribes of the Pyrenees. But in the fifth century there was the most stupendous illustration of this tendency, when all of Southern Europe was at last inundated by that northern deluge, and the effete Roman Empire was effaced.

The process had been a gradual one; had commenced, in fact, two centuries before the overthrow of the Roman Republic. But not until the fourth century, after the wicked old empire had espoused Christianity, did it become obvious that its foundations were undermined by this flood of barbarians. In 410 A. D., when the West-Goths, under Alaric, entered and sacked Rome, her power was broken. The roots no longer nourished the distant extremities in Britain and Gaul, and it was only a question of time when these, too, should succumb to the inflowing tide.

The Ostro-Goths — or East-Goths — in Northern Italy, and the Visigoths—or West-Goths—in Gaul, were setting up kingdoms of their own, under a Roman protectorate. The long period of peace in Spain was broken. The Pyrenees, with their warlike tribes, defended her for a time; but the Sueves and the Vandals—the latter a companion tribe of the Goths—had found an easier entrance by the sea on the east. They flowed down toward the south, and from thence across to the northern coast of Africa, which they colonized, leaving a memorial in Spain, in the lovely province of Andalusia, which was named after them—*Vandalusia*. But before the sacking of Rome a wave of the Gothic invasion had overflowed the Pyrenees, and Northern Spain had become a part of the Gothic kingdom in Gaul, with the city of Toulouse as its head.

A century of contact with Roman civilization had wrought great changes in this conquering race. They were untamed in strength, but realized the value of the civilities of life, and of intellectual superiority; and even strove to acquire some of the arts and accomplishments of the race they were invading. They were not yet acknowledged entire masters of Gaul and northern Spain. On condition of military service they had undisputed possession of their territory, with their own king, laws, and customs, but were nominally subjects of the Roman Emperor, Honorius.

Their attitude toward the Romans at this period cannot better be told than in the words of Ataulf himself (or Ataulfus, or Adolphus), whose interesting story will be briefly related. He says:

"It was my first wish to destroy the Roman name and erect in its place a Gothic Empire, taking to myself the place and the powers of Cæsar Augustus. But when experience taught me that the untamable barbarism of the Goths would not suffer them to live under the sway of law, and that the abolition of the institutions on which the state rested would involve the ruin of the state itself, I chose instead the glory of renewing and maintaining by Gothic strength the fame of Rome; preferring to go down to posterity as the restorer of that Roman power which it was beyond my power to replace."

These are not the words of a barbarian; although by the corrupt and courtly nobles in Rome he was considered one; but no doubt he towered far above the barbarous host whom he helped to lead into Rome in the year 410 A. D.

Ataulf was the brother-in-law of Alaric, and succeeded that great leader in authority after his death (410 A. D.).

At the time of the sacking of Rome this Gothic prince fell in love with Placidia, the sister of the Emperor Honorius; and after the fashion of his people, carried her away as his captive; not an unwilling one, we suspect, for we learn of her great devotion to her brave, strong wooer, with blond hair and blue eyes. Ataulf took his fair prize to the city of Narbonne in southern France, and made her his Queen. But when Constantius, a disappointed Roman lover of Placidia's, instigated Honorius to send an army against him and his Goths, he withdrew into Spain, and established his court with its rude splendor in the ancient city of Barcelona.

He seems to have had not an easy task between the desire to please his haughty Roman bride and, at the same time, to repel the charge of his people that he was becoming effeminate and Romanized; and, finally, so jealous did they become of her influence that Ataulf was assassinated in the presence of his wife, all his children butchered, and the proud Placidia compelled to walk barefoot through the streets of Barcelona.

Constantius, the faithful Roman lover, came with an army and carried back to Rome the royal widow, who married him and became the mother of Valentinian III., who succeeded his uncle Honorius as Emperor of Rome in 425 A. D., under the regency of Placidia during his infancy.

This romance, lying at the very root of a Gothic dynasty in Spain, marks the earliest beginnings of a line of Visigoth kings. Ataulf's successor removed his court to Toulouse in France, and Spain for many years remained only an outlying province of the Gothic kingdom; her turbulent northern tribes refusing to accept or to mingle with the strange intruders. When driven by the Romans from their mountain fastnesses the Basques, many of them, were at that time dispersed through southern and central France; which accounts for the presence of that race in France, before alluded to.

In the second half of the fifth century Attila, "the Scourge of God," swept down upon Europe with his Huns,—mysterious, terrible, as a fire out of heaven, and more like an army of demons than men,—destroying city after city, and driving the people before them, until they came to Orléans. There they met the combined Roman and Gothic armies. Theodoric, the Visigoth king, was killed on the battlefield. But to him, and to the Roman general Ætius, belongs the glory of the defeat of the Huns (451 A. D.).

It was Evaric, the son of this Theodoric, who finally completed the conquest of the Spanish Peninsula, and with him really commences the line of Visigoth kings in Spain, and the conversion of that country into a Gothic empire,* entirely independent of Rome.

The German *Franks*, under Clovis, established their kingdom in Gaul 481 A. D. The *Angles* and *Saxons* in 446 A. D. did the same in Britain. The *Ostrogoths* had their own kingdom in northern Italy and southern Gaul (Burgundy). So, with the *Visigoths* ruling in Spain, the " northern deluge " had in the fifth century practically submerged the whole of Europe, and above its dark waters showed only the somber wreck of a Roman empire.

From this fusing of Roman and Teutonic races there were to arise two types of civilization, utterly different in kind, the *Anglo-Saxon* and the *Latin*. In one the prevailing element, after the fusing was complete, was

---

* The famous Gothic code established by him still linger in much of Spanish jurisprudence.

to be the Teutonic; in the other, the Roman. Herein lies the difference between these two great divisions of the human family, and this is the germinal fact in the war raging to-day between Spain and the United States. It is a difference created not by the mastery of arms, but by the more efficient mastery of ideas.

When the Angles and Saxons conquered Britain, after a Roman occupation of over three hundred years, they swept it clean of Roman laws, literature, and civilization. Untamed pagan barbarians though they were, they had fine instincts and simple ideals of society and government, and they cast out the corrupt old empire, root and branch.

The Visigoths in Spain, more enlightened than they, already Christianized, and, perhaps, even superior in intelligence, were content in the words of Ataulf—" to renew and maintain by Gothic strength the fame of Rome." So they built upon the ruins of decaying institutions of a corrupt civilization, a kingdom which flourished with the enormous vitality drawn from the conquering race, which race was in turn conquered by Roman ideals.

So, in the conflict now existing between

Spain and the United States, we see the Spaniard, the child of the Romans; valorous, picturesque, cruel, versed in strategic arts, and with a savor of archaic wickedness which belongs to a corrupt old age. In the American we see the child of the simple Angles and Saxons, no less brave, but just, and with an enthusiasm and confiding integrity which seems to endow him with an imperishable youth.

CHAPTER VI.

THE story of Ulfilas, who Christianized the pagan Goths in the last half of the fourth century, is really the first chapter not alone in the history of Gothic civilization but in that of the German and English literatures; which, with their vast riches, had their origin in the strange achievement of Ulfilas. He had, while a boy, been captured by some Goths off the coast of Asia Minor, and was called by them " *Wulf-ilas* " (little wolf). In his desire to translate the Bible to his captors " Wulf-ilas reduced the Gothic language to writing. He had first to create an alphabet; taking twenty-two Roman letters, and inventing two more: the letter *w*, and still another for *th*. So while, after Constantine, the Christian religion was being adopted by the Roman Empire, and while its simple dogmas were being discussed and refined into a complicated and intricate system by men versed in Greek philosophy, and then formulated by minds trained in logic and rhetoric, the same religion was being spelled out in simple fashion by the Goths in central Europe from the book translated for them by Ulfilas.

All they found was that Jesus Christ was the beloved son of God and the Saviour of the world; that he was the long-promised Messiah, and to believe in him and to follow his teachings was salvation. They knew nothing of the Trinity nor of any theologic subtleties, and this was the simple faith which the Goths carried with them into the lands they conquered.

The Romans, who had spent three centuries in burning Christians and trying to obliterate the religion of Christ, were now its jealous guardians. They considered this "Arianism," as it was called, a blasphemous heresy, so shocking that they refused to call it Christianity at all. The history of the first century of the Gothic kingdom in Spain was therefore mainly that of the deadly strife between Arianism and Catholicism, or orthodoxy. The Goths could not discuss, for they were utterly unable to understand even the terms under discussion; but they could fight and lay down their lives for the faith which had done so much for them; and this they did freely and fiercely.

So the simple Gothic people were bewildered by finding themselves in the presence of a Christianity incomprehensible to them; a complicated, highly organized social order, equally incomprehensible; and a science and a literature of which they knew nothing. They might struggle for a while against this tide of superiority, but one by one they entered the fascinating portals of learning and of art, accepted the dogmas of learned prelates, and a few generations were sufficient to make them meek disciples of the older civilization.

The Spanish language fairly illustrates the result from this incongruous mingling of Roman and Gothic. It is said to be a language of Latin roots with a Teutonic grammar.

The Goths laid rough hands on the speech they consented to use, and the smooth, sonorous Latin was strangely broken and mixed with Gothic words and idioms; yet it became one of the most copious, flexible, and picturesque of languages, with a literature second to none.

In precisely the same way was the classic

old ruin of a Roman state re-enforced with a rough Gothic framework, and after centuries have hidden the joints and the scars with mosses and verdure, we have a picturesque and beautiful Spain!

But barbarous kings were fighting other things besides heresy. There were rebellions to put down; there were remnants of Sueves and of Roman power to drive out, and there were always the fierce mountain tribes who never mingled with any conquerors, nor had ever surrendered to anything but the Catholic faith.

There were intermarriages between the three Gothic kingdoms, in Burgundy, Gaul, and Spain, and the history of some of these royal families shows what wild passions still raged among the Goths, and what atrocities were strangely mingled with ambitious projects and religion.

Athanagild, one of the Visigoth kings, gave his daughter Brunhilde in marriage to the King of the Franks in Gaul. The story of this terrible Queen, stained with every crime, and accused of the death of no less than ten kings, comes to a fitting end when, we are told, that in her wicked old age she was tied to the tail of an unbroken horse and dragged over the stones of Paris (600 A. D.).

At this time Leovigild (570-587), the Visigoth King, was ruling Spain with a strong hand. He had assumed more splendor than any of his predecessors. He had erected a magnificent throne in his palace at Toledo, and his head, wearing the royal diadem, was placed on Spanish coins, which may still be seen. A daughter of the terrible Brunhilde, the Princess Ingunda, came over from France to become the wife of Ermingild, the son of the great King Leovigild, and heir to his throne.

All went smoothly until it was discovered that this fair Princess was a Catholic, and was artfully plotting to win her husband over to her faith from the faith of his fathers—Arianism.

Although Catholicism had made great inroads among their people, never before had it invaded the royal household. And when his son declared his intention to desert their ancient creed there commenced a terrible conflict between father and son, which finally led to Ermingild's open rebellion, and at last to his being beheaded by his father's order. But this crime against nature was in vain. Arianism had reached the limit of its life in Spain. Upon the death of Leovigild, his second son, Recared (587-601), succeeded to the throne, and one of his first acts was to abjure the old faith of the Gothic people, and Catholicism became the established religion of Spain.

CHAPTER VII.

TOLEDO, the capital of the Visigoth Kings, is the city about which cluster the richest memories of Spain in her heroic age. When Leovigild removed his capital there from Seville in the sixth century, it was already an ancient Jewish city, about which tradition had long busied itself. To-day, as it sits on the summit of a barren hill, one looks in vain for traces of its ancient Gothic splendor. But the spot where now stands a beautiful cathedral is hallowed by a wonderful legend, which Murillo made the subject of one of his great paintings. It is said that the Apostle St. James founded on that very spot the Church of *Santa Maria;* and that the Virgin, in recognition of the dedication to her, descended from heaven to present its Bishop, Ildofonso, with a marvelous chasuble. In proof of this miracle, doubting visitors are still shown the marks of Mary's footprint upon a stair in the chapel! However this may be, it is on this very spot that King Recared formally abjured Arianism; and preserved in a cloister of the cathedral may still be seen the "Consecration Stone," which reads: that the Church of Santa Maria, —built probably on the foundation of the older church,—was consecrated under "King Recared the Catholic, 587 A. D." It also tells of the councils of the Spanish Church held there—at one of which councils was the famous canon which decreed that all future Kings must swear they would show no mercy to "that accursed people"—meaning the Jews. It was these very Jews who had brought commercial success and created the enormous wealth of the city, from which it was now the duty of the pious Visigoth Kings to harry and hunt them as if they were frightened deer.

The Visigoth monarchy, although in many cases hereditary, was in fact elective. And the student of Spanish history will not find an orderly royal succession as in England and France. Disputes regarding the succession were not infrequent, and sometimes there will occur an interval with apparently no king at all, followed by another period when there are two—one ruling in the north and another in the south. "The King is dead—long live the King!" might do for France, but not for Spain.

During one of these periods of uncertainty, in the latter half of the seventh century, it is said that Leo, a holy man (afterward Pope), was told in a dream that the man who must wear the crown was then a laborer, living in the west, and that his name was Wamba. They traveled in search of this man almost to the borders of Portugal, and there they found the future candidate for the throne plowing in the field. The messengers, bowing before the plowman, informed him that he had been selected as King of Spain.

Wamba laughed, and said, "Yes, I shall be King of Spain when my pole puts forth leaves."

Instantly the bare pole began to bud, and in a few moments was covered with verdure!

In vain did Wamba protest. What could a poor man do in the face of such a miracle, and with a Spanish Duke pressing a poniard against his breast, and telling him to choose on the instant between a throne and a tomb!

The unhappy Wamba suffered himself to be borne in triumph to Toledo, and there to be crowned. And a very wise and excellent King did he make. He seemed fully equal to the difficult demands of his new position. A rebellion, fomented by an ambitious Duke Paul, who gathered about his standard all the banished Jews, was a very formidable affair. But Wamba put it down with a firm hand, and then, when it was over, treated the conspirators and rebels with marvelous clemency. When his reign was concluded he left a record of wisdom and sagacity rare in those days, in any land.

His taking off the stage was as remarkable as his coming on. He fell into a trance (October 14, 680), and after long insensibility it was concluded that the King was dying. According to a custom of the period Wamba's head was shaved, and he was clothed in the habit of a monk. The meaning of this was that if he died, he would, as was fitting, pass into the Divine presence in penitential garb. But if, peradventure, the patient survived, he was pledged to spend the rest of his life in that holy vocation, renouncing every worldly advantage.

So when, after a few hours, Wamba, in perfect health, opened his eyes, he found that instead of a King he was transformed into a Monk!

Whether this was a cunning device of this philosophic King to lay down the burdens which wearied him, and spend the rest of his days in tranquillity; or whether it was the work of the Royal Prince, who joyfully assumed the diadem which he had so unwillingly worn, nobody knows. But Wamba passed the remainder of his days in a monastery near Burgos, and the ambitious Ervigius reigned as his successor,

CHAPTER VIII.

THE Visigoth kingdom, which had stood for three centuries, had passed its meridian. It had created a magnificent background for historic Spain, and a heritage which would be the pride and glory of the proudest nation in Europe. The Goths had come as only rude intruders into that country; but to be descended from the Visigoth Kings was hereafter to be the proudest boast of the Spaniard. And the man who could make good such claim to distinction was a *Hidalgo;* or in its original form, *hijo-de-algo*—son of somebody.

But many generations of peace had impaired the rugged strength and softened the sinews of the nation. It was the beginning of the end when, at the close of the seventh century, there were two rival claimants to the throne; and while the vicious and cruel Witiza reigned at Toledo, Roderick, the son of Theodofred, also reigned in Andalusia. There had been a long struggle, during which it is said that Theodofred's eyes had been put out by his victorious rival, and his son Roderick had obtained assistance from the Greek Emperor at Byzantium in asserting his own claims. He succeeded in driving Witiza out of the country; and in 709,—" the last of the Goths,"—was crowned at Toledo, King of all Spain.

But the struggle was not over; and it was about to lead to a result which is one of the most momentous in the history, not alone of Spain,—nor yet of Europe,—but of *Christendom*. Witiza was dead, but his two sons, with a formidable following, were still trying to work the ruin of Roderick. A certain Count Julian, who, on account of his daughter Florinda, had his own wrongs to avenge, accepted the leadership of these rebels. The power of the Visigoths had extended across the narrow strait (cut by the Phenicians) over to the opposite shore, where Morocco seems to be reaching out in vain endeavor to touch the land from which she was long ago severed; and there, at Tangiers, this arch-traitor laid his plans and matured the scheme of revenge and treachery which had such tremendous results for Europe. With an appearance of perfect loyalty he parted from Roderick, who unsuspectingly asked him to bring him some hawks from Africa when he returned. Bowing, he said: " Sire, I will bring you such hawks as never were seen in Spain before."

For one hundred years an unprecedented wave of conquest had been moving from Asia toward the west. Mahommedanism, which was destined to become the scourge of Christendom, had subjected Syria, Mesopotamia. Egypt, and northern Africa, until it reached Ceuta—the companion Pillar to Gibraltar on the African coast.

At this point the Goths had stood, as a protecting wall beyond which the Asiatic deluge could not flow.

Count Julian was the trusted military commander of the Gothic garrisons in Morocco, as *Musa*, the oft-defeated Saracen leader, knew to his cost. As this Musa was one day looking with covetous eyes across at the Spanish Peninsula, he was suddenly surprised by a visit from Count Julian; and still more astonished when that commander offered to surrender to him the Gothic strongholds *Tangier*, *Arsilla*, and *Ceuta* in return for the assistance of the Saracen army in the cause of Witiza's sons against Roderick.

Amazed at such colossal treason, Musa referred Count Julian to his master the Khalif, at Damascus, who at once accepted his infamous proposition. In Spanish legend and history this man is always designated as *The Traitor*, as if standing alone and on a pinnacle among the men who have betrayed their countries.

Musa, half doubting, sent a preliminary force of about five hundred Moors under a chief named *Tarif*, to the opposite coast; and the Moors found, as was promised, that they might range at their own will and pleasure in that earthly paradise of Andalusia. The name of this Mussulman chief, Tarif, was given to the spot first touched by the feet of the Mahommedan, which was called *Tarifa;* and as Tarifa was afterward the place where customs were collected, the word *tariff* is an imperishable memorial of that event. In like manner Gibraltar was named *Gebel-al-Tarik*, (Mountain of Tarik) after the leader bearing that name, who was sent later by Musa with a larger force; which name has been gradually changed to its present form—Gibraltar.

Poor King Roderick, while still fighting to maintain his own right to the crown he wore, learned with dismay that his country was invaded by a horde of people from the African coast. Theodemir wrote to him: "So strange is their appearance that we might take them for inhabitants of the sky. Send me all the troops you can collect, without delay." The hawks promised by Count Julian had arrived!

The hour of doom had sounded for the last King of the Visigoths, and for his kingdom. There is a legend that a mysterious tower existed near Toledo, which was built by Hercules, soon after Adam, with the command that no king or lord of Spain should ever seek to know what it contained; instead of that it was the duty of each King to put a new lock upon its mysterious portal.

It is said that Roderick, perhaps in his extremity, resolved to disobey the command, and to discover the secret hidden in the Enchanted Tower. In a jeweled shrine in the very heart of the structure he came at last to a coffer of silver, "right subtly wrought," and far inside of that he reached the final mystery, —only this,—a white cloth folded between two pieces of copper. With trembling eagerness Roderick opened and found painted thereon men with turbans, carrying banners, with swords strung around their necks, and bows behind them, slung at the saddle-bow. Over these figures was written: " When this cloth shall be opened, men appareled like these shall conquer Spain, and be the lords thereof."

Such is the picturesque legend. Men with " turbans and banners and swords slung about their necks," were assuredly now in Andalusia, led by Tarik, who had literally burned his ships behind him, and then told his followers to choose between victory or death.

The two armies faced each other at a spot near Cadiz. It is said that Roderick, the degenerate successor of Alaric, went into battle in a robe of white silk embroidered with gold, sitting on a car of ivory, drawn by white mules. Tarik's men, who were fighting for victory or Paradise, overwhelmed the Goths; Roderick, in his flight, was drowned in the Guadalquivir, and his diadem of pearls and his embroidered robe were sent to Damascus as trophies.

Count Julian urged that the victory be immediately followed up by Musa before there was time for the Spaniards to rally. One after another the cities of Toledo, Cordova, and Granada capitulated, the persecuted Jews flocking to the new standard and aiding in the conquest of their oppressors.

As well might one have held back the Atlantic from rushing through that canal upon the isthmus, as to have stayed the inflowing of the Saracens through the breach made by " the Traitor," Count Julian! In less than two years Spain was a conquered province, rendering allegiance to the Khalif at Damascus, and the *Moor*,—as the followers of the Prophet in Morocco were called,—reigned in Toledo.

It was in the year 412 that Ataulfus, with his haughty bride Placidia, had established his Court at Barcelona, and Romanized Spain became Gothic Spain. In 711—just three centuries later—the Visigoth kingdom had disappeared as utterly beneath the Saracen flood as had its ill-fated King Roderick under the waters of the Guadalquivir; and fastened upon Christian Europe was a Mahommedan empire; an empire which all the combined powers of that continent have never since been able entirely to dislodge. From that illomened day in 709, when Tarif set foot on the Spanish coast, to this June of 1898, the Mahommedan has been in Europe; and remains to-day, a scourge and a blight in the territory upon which his cruel grasp still lingers.

CHAPTER IX.

TARIK and his twelve thousand Berbers,* or Moors, had at one stroke won the Spanish Peninsula. The banner of the Prophet waved over every one of the ancient and famous cities in Andalusia, and the turbaned army had marched through the stubborn north as far as the Spanish border. As Musa, intoxicated with success, stood at last upon the Pyrenees, he saw before him a vision of a subjugated Europe. The banner of the Prophet should wave from the Pyrenees to the Baltic! A mosque should stand where St. Peter's now stands in Rome! So, step by step, the Moslems pressed up into Gaul, and in 732 their army had reached Tours.

It was a moment of supreme peril for Christendom. But, happily, the Franks had what the Goths had not—a great leader. Charles Martel,—then *Maire du Palais*, and virtually King of France, instead of the feeble Lothair,

* The old Phenician name for the North African tribes, and plural of Iberia.

—led his Franks into what was to be one of the most decisive of the world's battles; a battle which would determine whether Europe should be Christian or Mahommedan.

The tide of infidel invasion had reached its limits. The strong right arm of Charles dealt such ponderous blows that the Moslems broke in confusion, and this savior of Christendom was thenceforth known as Charles Martel: " Karl of the Hammer."

After this crushing disaster at Tours the Moors realized that they were not invincible. Their vaulting ambition did not again try to overleap the Pyrenees; and they addressed themselves to settling affairs in their new territory.

It has been wisely said that if the Mahommedan state had been confined within the borders of Arabia, it would speedily have collapsed. Islam became a world-wide religion when it clothed itself with armor, and became a church militant. It was *conquest* which saved the faith of the Prophet. In its home in Asia the Empire of Mahommed was composed of hostile tribes and clans, and as it moved westward it gathered up Syrians, Egyptians, and the Berbers on the African coast, who, when Morocco was reached, were known as Moors. This strange, heterogeneous mass of humanity, all nourished from Arabia, was held together by two things: the *Koran* and the *sword*.

When conquest was exchanged for peaceful possession, all the internecine jealousies, the tribal feuds, and old hatreds burst forth, and the first fifty years of Moorish rule in Spain was a period of internal strife and disorder—Arabs and Moors were jealously trying to undermine each other; while the Arabs themselves were torn by factions representing rival clans in Damascus.

But a singular clemency was shown toward the conquered Spaniards. They were permitted to retain their own law and judges, and their own governors administered the affairs of the districts and collected the taxes. The rule of the conquering race bore upon the people actually less heavily than had the old Gothic rule. Jews and Christians alike were free to worship whom or what they pleased; but, at the same time, great benefits were bestowed upon those who would accept the religion of the Prophet. The slave class, which was very large and had suffered terrible cruelties under its old masters, was treated with especial mildness and humanity. There was a simple road to freedom opened to every man. He had only to say, "There is one God, and Mahommed is his Prophet," and on the instant he became a freeman!

Such gentle proselytizing as this speedily won converts, not alone among slaves but from all classes. The pacification of Spain by the Romans had required centuries; while only a few years sufficed to make of the vanquished in the southern provinces, a contented and almost happy people; not only reconciled, but even glad of the change of masters. Never was Andalusia so mildly, justly, and wisely governed as by her Arab conquerors.

The most delicate of all problems is that of dealing with a conquered race in its own land. That this should have been so wisely and so skillfully handled would be incomprehensible if this had been really, what it is always called, a Moorish conquest. But to be accurate, it was a Moorish invasion and a Saracen conquest!

The fierce Berber Moor contributed the brute force, which was wielded by Saracen intelligence.

The Saracens were the leaven which penetrated the whole sodden mass of Mahommedanism. With a civilization which had been ripening for centuries under Oriental skies,— rich in wisdom, learning, culture, science, and in art,—they had come into Europe, infidels though they were, to build up and not to destroy.

The Roman conquest of Spain had civilized a barbarous race. The Gothic conquest of Romanized Spain had converted an effete civilization into a strong semi-barbarism. Now again the Saracen had come from the East to convert a semi-barbarism into a civilization richer than any Spain had yet known, and, more than that, to hold up a torch of learning and enlightenment which should illumine Europe in the days of darkness which were at hand. Although this difference between Arab and Moor primarily existed, they became fused, and we shall speak of them only as Moors. But we should not lose sight of the fact that the superior intelligence which made the Moorish kingdom magnificent was from the land of the Prophet.

The Saracen dealt gently with the conquered Spaniard, not because his heart was tender and kind, but because he was crafty and wise, and knew when not to use force, in order to accomplish his ends. For the same reason he refrained from trying to break the spirit of the independent northern provinces, where the descendants of the old Visigoths—the Hidalgos ("sons-of-somebody")—proudly intrenched themselves in an attitude of defiance, making in time a clearly defined Christian north and Moslem south, with a mountain range (the Sierra Guadarrama) and a river (the Ebro) as the natural boundary line of the two territories. The Moor was a child of the sun. If the stubborn Goth chose to sulk, up among the chilly heights and on the bleak plains of the north, he might do so, and it was little matter if one Alfonso called himself "King of the Asturians," in that mountain-defended and sea-girt province. The fertile plains of Andalusia, and the banks of the Tagus and Guadalquivir, were all of Spain the Moor wanted for the wonderful kingdom which was to be the marvel of the Middle Ages.

CHAPTER X.

But, at the early period we are considering, the "Christian kingdom" was composed of a handful of men and women who had fled from the Moslems to the mountains of the Asturias. Its one stronghold was the cave of Covadonga, where Pelagius, or Pelayo, had gathered thirty men and ten women. Here, in the dark recesses of this cave,—which was approached through a long and narrow mountain pass, and entered by a ladder of ninety steps,—was the germ of the future kingdoms of Castile and Aragon, and also of the downfall of the Moor. An Arab historian said later: "Would to God the Moslems had extinguished that spark which was destined to consume the dominion of Islam in the north" and, he might have added, "*in Spain.*"

When Alfonso of Cantabria married the daughter of Pelayo in 751, the cave of Covadonga no longer held the insurgent band. He roused all the northern provinces against the Moors and gathered an army which drove them step by step further south, until he had pushed the Christian frontier as far as the great Sierra, so that the one-time Visigoth capital of Toledo marked the line of the Moslem border fortresses. Too scanty in numbers and too poor in purse to occupy the territory, Alfonso and his army then retreated to their mountains, there to enjoy the empty satisfaction of their conquest.

But the Moors in Andalusia had too many troubles of their own at that time to give much heed to Alfonso I. and his rebellious band hiding in the mountains. The Berbers and the Arabs on the African coast were jealous and antagonistic; the one was devout, credulous, and emotional; the other cool, crafty, and diplomatic. Suddenly the long-slumbering hatred burst into open revolt, and the Khalif sent thirty thousand Syrians to put down a formidable revolution in his African dominions.

In full sympathy with their kinsmen across the sea, the Moors in Spain began to realize that while that land had been won by twelve thousand Berbers, led by one Berber general, that the lion's share of the spoils had gone to the Arabs, who were carrying things with a high hand! There were signs of a general uprising, in concert with the revolution in Africa; and it looked as if the new territory was to be given up to anarchy; when suddenly all was changed.

The Khalif, who was the head of all the Mahommedan empire, was supposed to be the supreme ruler in spiritual and temporal affairs. But as his empire extended to such vast dimensions, he was obliged to delegate much of his temporal authority to others; so gradually it had become somewhat like that of the Pope. He was the supreme spiritual head, and only nominally supreme in affairs of state.

The family of *Omeyyad* had given fourteen Khalifs to the Mahommedan empire from 661 to 750; at which time the then reigning Omeyyad was deposed, and the second dynasty of Khalifs commenced, called *Abbaside*, after Abbas, an uncle of the Prophet.

Abd-er-Rahman was a Prince belonging to the deposed family of the Omeyyads. He was the only one of his family who escaped the exterminating fury of the Abbasides. There was no future for him in the east, so the thoughts of the ambitious youth turned to the west—to the newly won territory of Spain.

The coming of this last survivor of the Omeyyads to Andalusia is one of the romances of history, and was not unlike the coming of another young Pretender to Scotland, one thousand years later. It aroused the same wild enthusiasm, and as if by magic an army gathered about him, to meet the army of the Governor, Yusuf, which would resist him. Victory declared itself for the Prince, and he entered Cordova in triumph. Before the year had expired the dynasty of the Omeyyads—which was to stand for three centuries—was finally established, and its first king—Abd-er-Rahman—reigned at Cordova.

His hereditary enemies the Abbasides followed him to Spain, and found supporters among the disaffected. But it was in vain. The Abbaside army of invasion was utterly annihilated; and the qualities slumbering in this son of the Khalifs may be judged when we relate that the heads of the Abbaside leaders were put into a bag with descriptive labels attached to their ears, and sent to the reigning Khalif as a present.

This little incident does not seem to have

injured him in the estimation of Mansur, the new Khalif, who said to him: "Wonderful is this man! Such daring, wisdom, prudence! To throw himself into a distant land; to profit by the jealousies of the people; to turn their arms against one another instead of against himself; to win homage and obedience through such difficulties; and to rule supreme—lord of all! Of a truth there is not such another man!" Abd-er-Rahman (the Sultan, as he was called) merited this praise. He knew when to be cruel and when to show mercy; and how to hold scheming Arab chiefs, fierce, jealous Berbers, and vanquished Christians, and would placate or crucify as the conditions required.

CHAPTER XI.

CHARLEMAGNE was at this time building up his colossal empire. His Christian soul was mightily stirred by seeing an infidel kingdom set up in Andalusia; and when, in 777, the Saracen governor and two other Arab chiefs appealed to him for aid against the Omeyyad usurper, Abd-er-Rahman, he eagerly responded. His grandfather Charles Martel had driven these infidels back over the Pyrenees; now he would drive them out of Spain, and reclaim that land for Christianity!

His army never reached farther than Saragossa. He was recalled to France by a revolt of the recently conquered Saxons, and the "Battle of Roncesvalles" is the historic monument of the ill-starred attempt. The battle in itself was insignificant. No action of such small importance has ever been invested with such a glamour of romance, nor the theme of so much legend and poetry. It has been called the Thermopylæ of the Pyrenees, because of the personal valor displayed, and the tragic death of the two great Paladins (as the twelve Peers of Charlemagne were called) Roland and Olivier. The *Chanson de Roland* was one of the famous ballads in the early literature of Europe, and Roland and Olivier were to French and Spanish minstrelsy what the knights of King Arthur were to the English.

The simple story about which so much has been written and sung is this: As the retreating army of Charlemagne was crossing the Pyrenees, the rear of the army under Roland and Olivier was ambuscaded in the narrow pass of Roncesvalles by the Basques and exterminated to a man.

These Basques were the unconquerable mountain tribe of which we heard so much in the early history of Spain. They had been on guard for centuries, keeping the Franks back from the Pyrenees. They may have been acting under Saracenic influence when they exterminated the rear-guard of Charlemagne's army. But it was done, not because they loved the Saracen, but because they had a hereditary hatred for the Franks.

Mediæval Europe never tired of hearing of the Great Charles' lament over his Roland: "O thou right arm of my kingdom,—defender of the Christians,—scourge of the Saracens! How can I behold thee dead, and not die myself! Thou art exalted to the heavenly kingdom,—and I am left alone, a poor miserable King!"

CHAPTER XII.

THE tide which had flowed over southern Spain was a singular mixture of religious fervor, of brutish humanity, and refinements of wisdom and wickedness. No stranger and more composite elements were ever thrown together. Permanence and peace were impossible. Nothing but force could hold together elements so incongruous and antagonistic. As soon as the hand of Abd-er-Rahman I. was removed disintegration began. Clashing races, clans, and political parties had in a few years made such havoc that it seemed as if the Omeyyad dynasty was crumbling.

It might have been an Arab who said " he cared not who made the laws of his country, so he could write its songs." Learning, literature, refinements of luxury and of art had taken possession of the land, which seemed given up to the muses. When in 822 Abd-er-Rahman II. reigned, he did not trouble himself about the laws of his crumbling empire. The one man in whom he delighted was *Ziryab*. What Petronius was to Nero,* and Beau Brummel to George IV., that was Ziryab to the Sultan Abd-er-Rahman II., the elegant arbiter in matters of taste. From the dishes which should be eaten to the clothes which should be worn, he was the supreme judge; while at the same time he knew by heart and could "like an angel sing" one thousand songs to his adoring Sultan.

Even the Gothic Christians were seduced by these alluring refinements. They felt contempt for their old Latin speech and for their literature, with the tiresome asceticism it eternally preached. The Christian ideal had grown to be one of penance and mortification of the flesh, and to a few ardent souls these sensuous delights were an open highway to death eternal. *Eulogius* became the leader of this band of zealots. In lamenting the decadence of his people, he wrote, "hardly one in a thousand can write a decent Latin letter, and yet they indite excellent Arabic verse!" Filled with despairing ardor this man aroused a few kindred spirits to join him in a desper-

---

* See "Quo Vadis?"

ate attempt to awaken the benumbed conscience of the Christians. They could not get the Moslems to persecute them, but they might attain martyrdom by cursing the Prophet; then the infidels, however reluctant, would be compelled to behead them. This they did, and one by one perished, to no purpose. The Gothic Christians were not conscience-stricken as Eulogius supposed they would be, and there was no general uprising for the Christian faith.

In 912 the threatened ruin of the dynasty was arrested by the coming of another Abd-er-Rahman, third Sultan of that name. Rebellion was put down, and fifty years of wise and just administration gave solidity to the kingdom, which also then became a *Khalifate.*

The Abbaside Khalifs, after the deposition of the Omeyyads, had removed the Khalifate from Damascus to Baghdad. But the empire had extended too far west to revolve about that distant pivot. Abd-er-Rahman—perhaps remembering the old feud between his family and the Abbasides—determined to assume the spiritual headship of the western part of the empire. And thereafter, the Mahommedan empire—like the Roman—had two heads, an Eastern Khalif at Baghdad, and a Western Khalif at Cordova.

While thus extending his own power the Khalif was extinguishing every spark of rebellion in the south and driving the rebellious Christians back in the north, and at the same time he was clothing Cordova with a splendor which amazed and dazzled even the Eastern Princes who came to pay court to the great Khalif. His emissaries were everywhere collecting books for his library and treasure for his palaces. Cordova became the abode of learning, and the nursery for science, philosophy, and art, transplanted from Asia. The imagination and the pen of an arab poet could not have overdrawn this wonderful city on the Guadalquivir,—with its palaces, its gardens, and fountains,—its 50,000 houses of the aristocracy,—its 700 mosques,—and 900 public baths,—all adorned with color and carvings and tracery beautiful as a dream of Paradise. One hears with amazement of the great mosque, with its 19 arcades, its pavings of silver and rich mosaics, its 1293 clustered columns, inlaid with gold and lapis-lazuli, the clusters reaching up to the slender arches which supported the roof; the whole of this marvelous scene lighted by countless brazen lamps made from Christian bells, while hundreds of attendants swung censers, filling the air with perfume.

After the ravages of a thousand years travelers stand amazed to-day before the forest of columns which open out in endless vistas in the splendid ruin, calling up visions of the vanished glories of Cordova and the Great Khalif.

There is not time to tell of the city this Spanish Khalif built for his favorite wife, "The Fairest," and which he called "Hill of the Bride," upon which for fifteen years ten thousand men worked daily; nor of the four thousand columns which adorned its palaces, presents from emperors and potentates in Constantinople, Rome, and far-off Eastern states; nor of the ivory and ebony doors, studded with jewels, through which shone the sun, the light then falling on the lake of quicksilver, which sent back blinding, quivering flashes into dazzled eyes. And we are told of the thirteen thousand male servants who ministered in this palace of delight. All this, too, at a time when our Saxon ancestors were living in dwellings without chimneys, and casting the bones from the table at which they feasted into the foul straw which covered their floors; when a Gothic night had settled upon Europe, and blotted out civilization so completely that only in a part of Italy, and around Constantinople, did there remain a vestige of refinement!

It is said that when the embassy from Constantinople came bearing a letter to the Khalif, the courtier whose duty it was to read it was so awed by all this splendor that he fainted!

And yet the owner and creator of this fabulous luxury,—Sultan and Khalif of a dominion the greatest of his time, and with " The Fairest " for his adored wife,—when he came to die, left a paper upon which he had written that he could only recall fourteen days in which he had been happy.

CHAPTER XIII.

IN the north there was developing another and very different power. The descendants of the Visigoth Kings, making common cause with the rough mountaineers, had shared all their hardships and rigors in the mountains of the Asturias. Inured to privation and suffering, entirely unacquainted with luxury or even with the comforts of living, they had grown strong, and in a century after Alfonso I. had emerged from their mountain shelter and removed their court and capital from Oviedo to Leon, where Alfonso III. held sway over a group of barren kingdoms, poor, proud, but with *Hidalgo* and *Dons*, who were keeping alive the sacred fires of patriotism and of religion. This was the rough cradle of a Spanish nationality.

They had their own jealousies and fierce conflicts, but all united in a common hatred of the Moor. Though they did not yet dream of driving him out of their land, their brave leaders, Ramiro I. and Ordoño I. had been for years steadily defying and tormenting him with the kind of warfare to which they give its name—*guerrilla*—meaning "little wars."

While the Great Khalif was consolidating his Moorish kingdom and driving the Christians back into their mountains, the power of that people was being weakened by internal strifes existing between the three adjacent kingdoms—Leon, Castile, and Navarre. The headship of Leon was for years disputed by her ambitious neighbor Castile (so called because of the numerous fortified castles with which it was studded), under the leadership of one Fernando, Count of Castile.

There had been the usual lapse into anarchy and weakness after the Great Khalif's death. Andalusia always needed a master, and this she found in *Almanzor*, who was Prime Minister to one of the Khalif's feeble descendants. It was a sad day for the struggling kingdom in the north when this all-subduing man took the reins in his own hands, and left his young master to amuse himself in collecting rare manuscripts and making Cordova more beautiful.

This Almanzor, the mightiest of the soldiers of the Crescent since Tarik and Musa, proclaimed a war of faith against the Christians, who were obliged to forget their local dissensions and to try with their combined strength to save their kingdom from extermination. These were the darkest days to which they had yet been subjected. But for the death of Almanzor the ruin of the Christian state would have been complete. A monkish historian thus records this welcome event: " In 1002 died Almanzor, and was buried in hell."

The death of Almanzor was the turning point in the fortunes of the two kingdoms— that of the Moors and of the Christians.

Never again would Cordova be called the " Bride of Andalusia." The magnificence and the glory of the kingdom faded like the mist before the morning sun. Eight years after the death of Almanzor anarchy and ruin reigned in Cordova. The gentle, studious youth who was Khalif, was dragged with his only child to a dismal vault attached to the great mosque; and here, in darkness and cold and damp, sat the grandson of the first Great Khalif, his child clinging to his breast and begging in vain for food, his wretched father pathetically pleading with his jailers for just a crust of bread, and a candle to relieve the awful darkness.

The brutal Berbers now had their turn. The library, with its four hundred thousand priceless books, was in ashes. They were in the "City of the Fairest." Palace after palace was ransacked, and in a few days all that remained of its exquisite treasures of art was a heap of blackened stones (1010). The Christians drew their broken state closer together, and gathered themselves for a more aggressive warfare than any yet undertaken. The time when the Moors were in the throes of civil war was favorable. The three kingdoms of Asturias, Leon, and Castile were in 1073 united into one "kingdom of Castile," under Alfonso VI., who had already made great inroads upon the Moslem territory and laid many cities under tribute. With this event, the name *Castilian* comes into Spanish history, and from thenceforth that name represents all that is proudest, bravest, and most characteristic of the part of the race which traces a direct lineage from the ancient Visigoth Kings.

Alfonso had not misjudged his opportunity. He had traversed Spain with his army, and bathed in the ocean in sight of the " Pillars of Hercules." His great general Rodrigo Diaz, known as " My Cid, the Challenger," had cut another path all the way to Valencia, where he reigned as a sort of uncrowned king; and he will forever reign as crowned king in the realm of romance and poetry; the perfect embodiment of the knightly idea—the " Challenger," who, in defense of the faith, would stand before great armies and defy them to single combat! Whether " My Cid " ever did such mighty deeds as are ascribed to him, no one knows. But he stands for the highest ideal of his time. He was the " King Arthur " of Spanish history; and so valiantly did he serve the Christian cause that the Moors were driven to a most disastrous step. With the Cid in Valencia, with Alfonso VI. marching a victorious army through the Moslem territory, and with Toledo, the city of the ancient Visigoth Kings, repossessed, it looked as if, after almost four hundred years, the Christians were about to recover their land.

The Moors, thoroughly frightened, realizing how helpless they had grown, resolved upon a desperate measure.

There was, on the opposite African coast, a sect of Berber fanatics, fierce and devout, known as "saints," but which the Moors called *Almoravides*. Fighting for the faith was their occupation. What more fitting than to use them as a means of driving the infidel Christians out of Moslem territory!

They came, like a cloud of locusts, and settled upon the land. Yusuf, their general, led his men against Alfonso's Castilians October 23, 1086. Near Badajos the attack was made simultaneously in front and rear, crushing them utterly; Alfonso barely escaping with five hundred men. This was only the first of many other crushing defeats; the most disheartening of which was the one in 1099, when the Cid, fighting in alliance with Pedro, King of Aragon, was defeated near Gardia, on the seacoast. Then the great warrior's heart broke, and he died; and we are told he was clothed cap-à-pie in shining armor and placed upright on his good steed Bavieca, his trusty sword in his hand—and so he passed to his burial; his banner borne and guarded by five hundred knights. And we are also told the

Moors wonderingly watched his departure with his knights, not suspecting that he was dead.

The object of the Moors in inviting the odious Almoravides had been accomplished; the Christians had been driven out of Andalusia back into their own territory; but their African auxiliaries were too well pleased with their new abode to think of leaving it. One by one the Moorish Princes were subdued by the men whose aid they had invoked, until a dynasty of the Almoravides was fastened upon Spain. To the refined Spanish Arabs contact with these savages from the desert was a terrible scourge, and so far as they were able they withdrew into communities by themselves, leaving these African locusts to devour their substance and dim their glory.

But luxury was not favorable to the invaders. In another generation their martial spirit was gone and they had become only ignorant, sodden voluptuaries; and when the Christians once more renewed their attacks, they failed to repel them as Yusuf had done thirty years before.

There was another fanatical sect, beyond the Atlas range in Africa, which had long been looking for a coming Messiah, whom they called the *Mahdi*. They were known as the *Alhomades*. A son of a lamp-lighter in the Mosque of Cordova one day presented himself before the Alhomades, and announced that he was the great *Mahdi*, who was divinely appointed to lead them, and to bring happiness to all the earth.

The path this *Mahdi* desired to lead them was first to Morocco, there to subdue the Almoravides in their own land, and thence to Spain. In a short time this entire plan was realized. The Mahdi's successor was Emperor of Morocco, and by the year 1150 included in his dominion was all of Mahommedan Spain! The Spanish Arabs, when they were fighting Alfonso II. and the "Cid," did not anticipate this disgraceful downfall from people of their own faith. They abhorred these Mahommedan savages, and drew together still closer for a century more in and about their chosen refuge of Granada.

In the early part of the thirteenth century the Emperor of Morocco made such enormous preparations for the occupation of Spain that a larger design upon Europe became manifest. Once more Christendom was alarmed; not since Charles Martel had the danger appeared so great. The Pope proclaimed a Crusade, this time not into Palestine, but Spain.

An army of volunteers from the kingdom of Portugal and from southern France re-enforced the great armies of the Kings of Castile, Aragon, and Navarre. The Crusaders, as they called themselves, assembled at Toledo July 12, 1212, under the command of Alfonso IX., King of Castile. The power of the Alhomades was broken, and they were driven out of Spain. The once great Mahommedan Empire in that country was reduced to the single province of Granada, where the Moors intrenched themselves in their last stronghold. For nearly three centuries the Crescent was going to wave over the kingdom of Granada; but it was to shine in only the pale light of a waning crescent, until its final extinction in the full light of a Christian day.

CHAPTER XIV.

A GREAT change had been wrought in Europe. The Crusades had opened a channel through which flowed from the East reviving streams of ancient knowledge and culture over the arid waste of mediævalism. France and England had awakened from their long mental torpor, Paris was become the center of an intellectual revival. In England, Roger Bacon, in his "Opus Majus," was systematizing all existing knowledge and laying a foundation for a more advanced science and philosophy for the people, who had only recently extorted from their wicked King John the great charter of their liberties.

It was just at this period, when the door had suddenly opened ushering Europe into a new life, that the Christian cause in Spain triumphed; and, excepting in the little kingdom of Granada, the Cross waved from the Pyrenees to the sea. After more than four centuries of steadfast devotion to that object, the descendants of the Visigoth Kings had come once more into their inheritance.

They found it enriched, and clothed with a beauty of which their ancestors could never have dreamed. These Spaniards had learned their lesson of valor in the north, and they had learned it well. Now in the land of the Moor, dwelling in the palaces they had built, and gazing upon masterpieces of Arabic art and architecture which they had left, they were to learn the subtle charm of form and color, and the fascination which music and poetry and beauty and knowledge may lend to life. As they drank from these Moorish fountains the rugged warriors found them very sweet; and they discovered that there were other pleasures in life beside fighting the Moors and nursing memories of the Cid and their vanished heroes.

The territory of Ferdinand III., King of Castile (1230-52), extended now from the Bay of Biscay to the Guadalquivir. The ancient city of Seville was chosen as his capital. It was a far cry from the "Cave of Covadonga" to the Moorish palace of the "Alcazar," where dwelt the pious descendant of Pelayo! The first act of Fernando III. was to convert the

Mosque at Seville into a cathedral, which still stands with its Moorish bell-tower, the beautiful "Giralda." There may also be seen to-day over one of its portals a stuffed crocodile, which was sent alive to King Ferdinand by the Sultan of Egypt. And within the cathedral, in a silver urn with glass sides, the traveler may also gaze to-day upon the remains of this "Saint Ferdinand" clothed in royal robes, and with a crown upon his head.

Spain had begun to lift up her head among the other nations of Europe. To defeat the Crescent was the highest ideal of that chivalric age. Spain, longer than any other nation, had fought the Mahommedan. It had been her sole occupation for four centuries, and now she had vanquished him, and driven him into the mountains of one of her smallest provinces, there to hide from the Spaniards as they had once hidden from the Moors in the North. This was a passport to the honor and respect of other Christian nations. She was Spain "the Catholic" —the loved and favorite child of the Church—and great monarchs in England, France, and Germany bestowed their sons and daughters upon her kings and princes. Poor though she was in purse, and somewhat rude yet in manners, she held up her head high in proud consciousness of her aristocratic lineage, and her unmatched championship of Christianity.

We realize how close had become the tie binding her to other nations when we learn that King Ferdinand III. was the grandson of Queen Eleanor of England (daughter of Henry II.), and that Louis IX. of France, that other royal saint, was his own cousin; and also that his wife Beatrix, whom he brought with him to Seville, was daughter of the Emperor of Germany.

The deep hold which Arabic life and thought had taken upon their conquerors was shown when Alfonso X., son of Ferdinand, came to the throne. So in love was he with learning and science that he let his kingdom fall into utter confusion while he busied himself with a set of astronomical tables upon which his heart was set and in holding up to ridicule the Ptolemaic theory. If he had given less thought to the stars, and more to the humble question as to who was to be his successor, it would have saved much strife and suffering to those who came after him.

While the Moslems were building up their kingdom and making of their capital city a second and even more beautiful Cordova, there was a partial truce with the Moors in Granada. Moors and Christians were enemies still; the hereditary hatreds were only lulled into temporary repose. But Christian knights who were handsome and gallant might love and woo Moorish maidens who were beautiful; and, as a writer has intimated, love became the business and war the pastime of the Spaniard in Andalusia. Spain was unconsciously inbibing the soft, sensuous charm of the civilization she was exterminating; and the peculiar rhythm of Spanish music, and the subtle picturesqueness which makes the Spanish people unique among the other Latin nations of Europe, came, not from her Gothic, nor her Roman, nor her Phenician ancestry, but from the plains of Arabia; and the guitar and the dance and the castanet, and the charm and the coquetry of her women, are echoes from that far-off land of poetry and romance. Not so the bull-fight! Would you trace to its source that pleasant pastime, you must not go to the East; the Oriental was cruel to man, but not to beast. He would have abhorred such a form of amusement, for the origin of which we must look to the barbarous Kelt; or perhaps, as is more probable, to the mysterious Iberians, since among the Latin peoples of Europe bull-fighting is found in Spain alone. Well was it for Spain that her rough, untutored ancestors were kept hiding in the mountains for centuries, while that brilliant Oriental race planted their Peninsula thick with the germs of high thinking and beautiful living.

As the spider, after his glistening habitation has been destroyed by some ruthless footstep, goes patiently to work to rebuild it, so the Moor in Granada, with his imperishable instinct for beauty, was making of his little kingdom the most beautiful spot in Europe. The city of Granada was lovelier than Cordova; its Alhambra more enchanting than had been the palaces in the "City of the Fairest." This citadel, which is fortress and palace in one, still stands like the Acropolis, looking out upon the plain from its lofty elevation. Volumes have been written about its labyrinthine halls and corridors and courts, and the amazing richness of decoration, which still survives—an inexhaustible mine for artists and a shrine for lovers of the beautiful. But Granada cultivated other things besides the art of beauty. Nowhere in Europe was there in the thirteenth and fourteenth centuries such advanced thinking, and a knowledge so akin to our own to-day, as within the borders of that Moorish kingdom.

CHAPTER XV.

THERE were other reasons beside the growing peacefulness of the Spaniards why Granada was left to develop in comparative security for two centuries. It was impossible that adjacent ambitious kingdoms, such as Navarre, Castile, Aragon, Leon, and Portugal, with indefinite and disputed boundaries, and, on account of intermarriages between the kingdoms, with indefinite and disputed successions, should ever be at peace. In the perpetual strife and warfare which prevailed on account of royal European alliances, the fate of foreign princes and princesses were often involved, and hence European states stood ready to take a hand.

Castile and Aragon had gradually absorbed the smaller states, excepting Portugal on the one side and Navarre on the other. The history of Spain at this time is a history of the struggles of these two states for supremacy. The most eventful as well as the most lurid period of this prolonged civil war was while Pedro the Cruel was king of Castile, 1350-69. This Spanish Nero, when sixteen years old, commenced his reign by the murder of his mother. A catalogue of his crimes is impossible. Enough to say that assassination was his remedy, and means of escape, from every entanglement in which his treacheries involved him. It was the unhappy fate of Blanche de Bourbon, sister of Charles V., King of France, to marry this King of Castile, and when he refused to live with her and had her removed from his palace the Alcazar to a fortress, and finally poisoned her, the French King determined to avenge the insult to his royal house. He allied himself with the King of Aragon to destroy Pedro, with whom the King of Aragon was of course at war.

Edward, the " Black Prince," was then brilliantly invading France and extending the kingdom of his father Edward III. He was the kinsman of Pedro, and when appealed to by his cousin for aid in protecting his kingdom from the King of Aragon and his French allies, Edward gallantly consented to help him; and in the spring of 1367, for the second time, a splendid army advanced through the

Pass at Roncesvalles, and a great battle. worthy of a better cause, was fought and won.

So this most atrocious king—perhaps excepting Richard III. of England, whom he resembled—had for his champion the victor of Cressy and Poictiers. He was restored to his throne, which had been usurped by his brother Enrique (or Henry), but in a personal encounter with Enrique soon after (which was artfully brought about by the famous Breton knight, Bertrand du Guesclin), he met a deserved fate (1369).

Constanza, the daughter of Pedro the Cruel, had been married to John of Gaunt (Duke of Lancester), brother of the Black Prince and son of Edward III. As Constanza was the great-grandmother of Isabella I. of Spain, so in the veins of that revered Queen there flowed the blood of the Plantagenets, as well as that of Pedro the Cruel!

Because of the number of doubtful pretenders always existing in Spain, disputes about the royal succession also always existed. Such a dispute now led to a long war with Portugal, where King Fernando had really the most valid hereditary claim to the throne made vacant by Pedro's death. If his right had been acknowledged, Portugal and Spain would now be united; Isabella would have remained only a poor and devout princess, and would never have had the power to win a continent for the world. So impossible is it to remove one of the links forged by fate, that we dare not regret even so monstrous a reign as that of Pedro the Cruel!

Enrique's right to the vacant throne of his brother had two disputants. Besides the King of Portugal, John of Gaunt, who had married the lady Constanza,—by virtue of her rights as daughter of Pedro,—claimed the crown of Castile. This Plantagenet was actually proclaimed King of Castile and Leon (1386). For twenty-five years he vainly strove to come into his kingdom as sovereign; but finally compromised by giving his young daughter Catherine to the boy "Prince of Asturias," the heir to the throne. He was obliged to content himself by thus securing to his child the long-coveted prize. And it was this Catherine, who at fourteen was betrothed to a boy of nine, who was the grandmother of Isabella, Queen of Castile.

When such was the private history of those

highest in the land we can only imagine what must have been that of the rest. Feudalism, which was a part of Spain's Gothic inheritance, had always made that country one of its strongholds, and chivalry had nowhere else found so congenial a soil. There was no great artisan class, as in France, creating a powerful " bourgeoisie "; no " guilds," or simple " burghers," as in Germany, stubbornly standing for their rights; no " boroughs " and " town meetings," where the people were sternly guarding their liberties, as in England.

The history of other nations is that of the struggles of the common people against the tyranny of kings and rulers. If there were any " common people " in Spain, they were so effaced that history makes no mention of them. We hear only of kings and great barons and glorious knights; and their wonderful deeds and their valor and prowess—excepting in the wars with the Moors—were always over boundary-lines and successions, or personal quarrels more or less disgraceful, with never a single high purpose or a principle involved. It was all a gay, ambitious pageant, adorned by a mantle of chivalry, and made sacred by the banner of the Cross. In the history of no other European country do we see a great state develop under despotism so unredeemed by wholesome ideals, and so unmitigated and unrestrained by gentle human impulses.

CHAPTER XVI.

JUAN II., the son of the young Catherine and the boy prince of the Asturias, died in 1454, and his son Enrique (or Henry) IV. was King of Castile. When, after some years, Henry was without children, and with health very infirm, his young sister Isabella unexpectedly found herself the acknowledged heir to the throne of Castile. She suddenly became a very important young person. The old King of Portugal was a suitor for her hand, and a brother of the King of England, and also a brother of the King of France, were striving for the same honor. But Isabella had very decided views of her own. Her hero was the young Ferdinand of Aragon, and heir to that throne. She resisted all her brother's efforts to coerce her, and finally took the matter into her own hands by sending an envoy to her handsome young lover to come to her at Valladolid, with a letter telling him they had better be married at once.

Accompanied by a few knights disguised as merchants, Ferdinand, pretending to be their servant, during the entire journey waited on them at table and took care of their mules. He entered Valladolid, where he was received by the Archbishop of Toledo, who was in the conspiracy, and was by him conveyed to Isabella's apartments. We are told that when he entered someone exclaimed: *Ese-es, Ese-es* (that is he); and the escutcheon of that knight has ever since borne a double *S. S.*, which sounds like this exclamation.

The marriage was arranged to take place in four days. An embarrassment then occurred of which no one had before thought. Neither of them had any money. But someone was found who would lend them enough for the wedding expenses, and so on the 19th of October, 1469, the most important marriage ever yet consummated in Spain took place—a marriage which would forever set at rest the rivalries between Castile and Aragon, and bring honors undreamed of to a united Spain.

Isabella was fair, intelligent, accomplished, and lovely. She was eighteen and her boy husband was a year younger. Of course her royal brother stormed and raged. But, of course, it did no good. In five years from that time (1474) he died, and Isabella, royally attired, and seated on a white palfrey, proceeded to the throne prepared for her, and was there proclaimed "Queen of Castile." At the end of another five years, Ferdinand came into his inheritance. His old father, Juan II., King of Aragon and Navarre, died in 1479, and Castile, Aragon, and Navarre— all of Spain except Portugal and Granada— had come under the double crown of Ferdinand and Isabella.

The war with Portugal still existed, and their reign began in the midst of confusion and trouble, but it was brilliant from the outset. Ferdinand had great abilities and an ambition which matched his abilities. Isabella, no less ambitious than he, was more far-reaching in her plans, and always saw more clearly than Ferdinand what was for the true glory of Spain. With infinite tact she softened his asperities, and disarmed his jealousy, and ruled her "dear lord," by making him believe he ruled her.

A joint sovereignty, with a man so grasping of power and so jealous of his own rights, required self-control and tact in no ordinary measure. It was agreed at last that in all public acts Ferdinand's name should precede hers; and although her sanction was necessary, his indignation at this was abated by her promise of submission to his will. The court of the new sovereigns was established at Seville, and they took up their abode in that palace so filled with associations both Moorish and Castilian—the Alcazar. From the very first Isabella's powerful mind grappled every public question, and she gave herself heart and soul to what she believed was her divine mission—the building up of a great Catholic state. Isabella's devout soul was sorely troubled by the prevalence of Judaism in her kingdom. She took counsel with her confessor, and also with the Pope, and by their advice a religious tribunal was established at Seville in 1483, the object of which was to inquire of heretics whether they were willing to renounce their faith and accept Christianity. The head of this tribunal, which was soon followed by others in all the large cites, was a Dominican friar called *Torquemada*. He was known as the "Inquisitor General." Inaccessible to pity, mild in manners, humble in demeanor, yet swayed openly by a sense of duty, this strange being was so cruel that he seems like an incarnation of the evil principle. At the tribunal in Seville alone it is said that in thirty-six years four thousand victims were consigned to the flames, besides the thousands more who endured living deaths by torture, mutilation, and nameless sufferings.

Humanity shudders at the recital! And yet this monstrous tribunal was the creation of one of the wisest and gentlest of women, who believed no rigors could be too great to save people from eternal death! And, in her misguided zeal, she emptied her kingdom of a people who had helped to create its prosperity, and drove the most valuable part of her population into France, Italy, and England, there to disseminate the seeds of a higher culture and intelligence which they had imbibed from contact with the Moors, who had treated them with such uniform tolerance and gentleness.

The kingdom of Granada was now at the height of its splendor. Its capital city was larger and richer than any city in Spain. Its army was the best equipped of any in Europe. The Moorish king, a man of fiery temper, thought the time had come when he might defy his enemy by refusing to pay an annual tribute to which his father had ten years before consented. When Ferdinand's messenger, in 1476, came to demand the accustomed tribute, he said, " Go tell your master the kings who pay tribute in Granada are all dead. Our mints coin nothing but sword-blades now."

The cool and crafty Ferdinand prepared his own answer to this challenge. The infatuated King Abdul-Hassan followed up his insult by capturing the Christian fortress of Zahara. His temper was not at the best at this time on account of a war raging in his own household. His wife Ayesha was fiercely jealous of a Christian captive whom he had also made his wife. She had become his favorite Sultana, and was conspiring to have her own son supplant Boabdil, the son of Ayesha, the heir to the throne. In his championship of Zoraya and her son, Abdul-Hassan imprisoned Ayesha and Boabdil, whom he threatened to disinherit. We are shown to-day the window in the Alhambra from which Ayesha lowered Boabdil in a basket, telling him to come back with an army and assert his rights. Suddenly, while absorbed by this smaller war, news came that Alhama, their most impregnable fortress, only six leagues from the city of Granada, had been captured by Ferdinand's army. It was the key to Granada. Despair was in every soul. The air was filled with wailing and lamentation. " Woe, woe is me, Alhama! " " Ay de mi, Alhama! " Indignant with their old king, who had brought destruction upon them, when Boabdil came with his army of followers, they flocked about him—" El Rey Chico! " (the boy king) as they called him. Abdul Hassan was forced to fly, and Boabdil reigned over the expiring kingdom. It was a brief and troubled reign.

In the famous " Court of the Lions " in the Alhambra, visitors are shown to-day the blood-stains left by the celebrated massacre of the " Abencerrages." The Abencerrages had supported the claim of Ayesha's rival, Zoraya; and it is said that Boabdil invited the Princes of this clan, some thirty in number, to a friendly conference in the Alhambra, and there had them treacherously beheaded at the fountain.

But whether this blood-stain upon his memory is as doubtful as those upon the stones at the fountain, seems an open question.

So stubborn was the defense, it appeared sometimes as if the reduction of Granada would have to be abandoned. Isabella's courage and faith were sorely tried. But the brave Queen infused her own courage into the flagging spirits of her husband, and kept alive the enthusiasm of the people; and at last,—on the 2d of January, 1492,—the proud city capitulated. Boabdil surrendered the keys of the Alhambra to Ferdinand—the silver cross which had preceded the King throughout the war gleamed from a high tower; and from the loftiest pinnacle of the Alhambra waved the banners of Castile and Aragon.

The conflict which had lasted for 781 years was over. The death of Roderick and the fall of the Goths was avenged, and Christendom, still weeping for the loss of Constantinople, was consoled and took heart again.

CHAPTER XVII.

THE reduction of Granada had required eleven years, and had drained the kingdom of all its resources. It is not strange that Isabella should have had no time to listen seriously to a threadbare enthusiast asking for money and ships for a strange adventure! To have grown old and haggard in pressing an unsuccessful project is not a passport to the confidence of Princes. But the gracious Queen had promised to listen to him when the war with the Moors was concluded. So now Columbus sought her out at Granada; and it is a strange scene which the imagination pictures—a shabby old man pleading with a Queen in the halls of the Alhambra for permission to lift the veil from an unsuspected Hemisphere; artfully dwelling upon the glory of planting the Cross in the dominions of the Great Khan! The cool, unimaginative Ferdinand listened contemptuously; but Isabella, for once opposing the will of her " dear lord," arose and said, "The enterprise is mine. I undertake it for Castile." And on the 3d of August, 1492, the little fleet of caravels sailed from the mouth of the same river whence had once sailed the "ships of Tarshish," laden with treasure for King Solomon and "Hiram, King of Tyre." A union with Portugal—the land of the Lusitanians and of Sertorius—was all that was now required to make of the Spanish Peninsula one kingdom. This Isabella planned to accomplish by the marriage of her oldest daughter, Isabella, with the King of Portugal. Her son John, heir to the Spanish throne, had died suddenly just after his marriage with the daughter of Maximilian, Emperor of Germany.

This terrible blow was swiftly followed by another, the death of her daughter Isabella, and also that of the infant which was expected to unite the kingdoms of Portugal and Spain. The succession of Castile and Aragon now passed to Joanna, her second daughter, who had married Philip, Archduke of Austria and son of Maximilian, an unfortunate child who seemed on the verge of madness.

Isabella's youngest daughter, Catherine, became the wife of Henry VIII. of England.

Happily the mother did not live to witness this child's unhappiness; but her heart-breaking losses and domestic griefs were greater than she could bear. The unbalanced condition of Joanna, upon whom rested all hopes, was undermining her health. The results of the expedition of Columbus had exceeded the wildest dreams of romance. Gold was pouring in from the West enough to pay for the war with the Moors many times over, and for all wars to come. Spain, from being the poorest, had suddenly become the richest country in Europe; richest in wealth, in territory, and in the imperishable glory of its discovery. But Isabella,—who had been the instrument in this transformation,—who had built up a firm united kingdom and swept it clean of heretics, Jews, and Moors,—was still a sad and disappointed woman, thwarted in her dearest hopes; and on the 26th of November, 1504, she died leaving the fruits of her triumphs to a grandson six years old.

This infant Charles was proclaimed King of Castile under the regency of his ambitious father, the Archduke of Austria, and his insane mother. The death of the Archduke and the incapacity of Joanna in a few years gave to Ferdinand the control of the two kingdoms for which he had contended and schemed, until his own death in 1516, when the crowns of Castile and Aragon passed to his grandson, who was proclaimed Charles I., King of Spain.

A plain, sedate youth of sixteen was called from his home in Flanders to assume the crowns of Castile and Aragon. Silent, reserved, and speaking the Spanish language very imperfectly, the impression produced by the young King was very unpromising. No one suspected the designs which were maturing under that mask; nor that this boy was planning to grasp all the threads of diplomacy in Europe, and to be the master of kings.

In 1517 Maximilian died, leaving a vacant throne in Germany to be contended for by the ambitious Francis I. of France and Maximilian's grandson, Charles.

It was a question of supremacy in Europe. So the successful aspirant must win to himself Leo X., Henry VIII. and his great minister Wolsey, and after that the Electors of Germany. It required consummate skill. Francis I. was an able player. The astute Wolsey made the moves for his master Henry VIII., keeping a watchful eye on Charles, "that young man who looks so modest, and soars so high"; while Leo X., unconscious of the coming Reformation, was craftily aiding this side or that as benefit to the Church seemed to be promised.

But that "modest young man" played the strongest game. Charles was, by the unanimous vote of the Electors, raised to the imperial throne; and the grandson of Isabella, as Charles I. of Spain and Charles V. of Germany, possessed more power than had been exercised by any one man since the reign of Augustus. The territory over which he had dominion in the New World was practically without limit. Mexico surrendered to Cortez (1521) and Peru to Pizarro (1532); Ponce de Leon was in Florida and de Soto on the banks of the Mississippi; while wealth, fabulous in amount, was pouring into Spain, and from thence into Flanders.

The history of Charles belongs, in fact, more to Europe than to Spain. No slightest tenderness seems to have existed in his cold heart for the land of Isabella, which he seemed to regard simply as a treasury from which to draw money for the objects to which he was really devoted. So, in fact, Spain was governed by an absolute despot who was Emperor of Germany, where he resided, and she visibly declined from the strength and prosperity which had been created by the wise and personal administration of Ferdinand and Isabella.

The Cortes, where the deputies had never been allowed the privilege of debate, had been at its best a very imperfect expression of popular sentiment; and now was reduced to a mere empty form. Abuses which had been corrected under the vigilant personal administration of two able and patriotic sovereigns returned in aggravated form. Misrule and disorder prevailed, while their King was absorbed in the larger field of European politics and diplomacy.

The light in which Spain shines in this, which is always accounted her most glorious period, was that of Discovery and Conquest, and the enormous wealth coming therefrom; all of which was bestowed by that shabby adventurer and suppliant at the Alhambra, in whom Isabella alone believed, and who, after enriching Spain beyond its wildest expectations, was permitted to die in poverty and neglect at Valladolid in 1506! History has written its verdict: imperishable renown to Columbus, Balboa, Magellan, and the navigators who dared such perils and won so much; and eternal infamy to the men who planted a bloodstained Cross in those distant lands. The history of the West Indies, of Mexico, and Peru is unmatched for cruelty in the annals of the world; and Isabella's is the only voice that was ever raised in defense of the gentle, helpless race which was found in those lands.

The Reformation, which had commenced in Germany with the reign of Charles V., had assumed enormous proportions. Charles, who was a bigot with "heart as hard as hammered iron," was using with unsparing hand the Inquisition, that engine of cruelty created by his grandmother. And while his captains, the "conquistadors," were burning and torturing in the West, he was burning and torturing in the East. His entire reign was occupied in a struggle with his ambitious rival Francis I., and another and vain struggle with the followers of Luther.

He had married Isabel, the daughter of the King of Portugal. Philip, his son and heir, was born in 1527. The desire of his heart was to secure for this son the succession to the imperial throne of Germany. To this the electors would not consent. He was defeated in the two objects dearest to his heart: the power to bequeath this imperial possession to Philip, and the destruction of Protestantism. So this most powerful sovereign since the day of Charlemagne felt himself ill-used by Fate. Weary and sick at heart, in the year 1556 he abdicated in favor of Philip. The Netherlands was his own to bestow upon his son, as that was an inheritance from his father, the Archduke of Austria. So the fate of Philip does not seem to us so very heart-breaking, as, upon the abdication of his father, he was King of Spain, of Naples, and of Sicily; Duke of Milan; Lord of the Netherlands and of the Indies, and of a vast portion of the American continent stretching from the Atlantic to the Pacific!

Such was the inheritance left to his son by the disappointed man who carried his sorrows to the monastery at St. Yuste, where the austerities and severities he practiced finally cost him his life (1558). But let no one suppose that these penances were on account of cruelties practiced upon his Protestant subjects! From his cloister he wrote to the inquisitors adjuring them to show no mercy; to deliver all to the flames, even if they should recant; and the only regret of the dying penitent was that he had not executed Luther!

CHAPTER XVIII.

PHILIP established his capital at Madrid, and commenced the Palace of the Escurial, nineteen miles distant, which stands to-day as his monument. His coronation was celebrated by an *auto-da-fé* at Valladolid, which it is said "he attended with much devotion." One of the victims, an officer of distinction, while awaiting his turn said to him: "Sire, how can you witness such tortures?" "Were my own son in your place I should witness it," was the reply; which was a key to the character of the man.

He asserted his claim through his mother, the Princess Isabel of Portugal, to the throne of that country, and after a stubborn contest with the Lusitanians, the long-desired union of Spain and Portugal was accomplished. This event was celebrated by Cervantes in a poem which extravagantly lauds his sovereign. Henry VIII. had been succeeded in England by Mary, daughter of his unhappy

Queen, Catherine of Aragon, who, it will be remembered, was the daughter of Ferdinand and Isabella. Mary had inherited the intense religious fervor and perhaps the cruel instincts of her mother's family, and she quickly set about restoring Protestant England to the Catholic faith. Philip saw in a union with Mary and a joint sovereignty over England, such as he hoped would follow, an immense opportunity for Spain. The marriage took place with great splendor, and in the desire to please her handsome husband, of whom she was very fond, she commenced the work which has given her the title, " Bloody Mary." In vain were human torches lighted to lure Philip from Spain, where he lingered. She did not win his love, nor did Philip reign conjointly with his royal consort in England. Mary died in 1558, and her Protestant sister Elizabeth, daughter of Anne Boleyn, was Queen of England.

Philip had made up his mind that Protestantism should be exterminated in his kingdom of the Netherlands. He could not go there himself, so he looked about for a suitable instrument for his purpose. The Duke of Alva was the man chosen. He was appointed Viceroy, with full authority to carry out the pious design. Heresy must cease to exist in the Netherlands. The arrival of Alva, clothed with such despotic powers, and the atrocities committed by him, caused the greatest indignation in the Netherlands. The Prince of Orange, aided by the Counts Egmont and Horn, organized a party to resist him, and a revolution was commenced which lasted for forty years, affording one of the blackest chapters in the history of Europe. The name of Alva stands at the head of the list of men who have wrought desolation and suffering in the name of religon. The other European states protested, and Elizabeth, in hot indignation, gave aid to the persecuted states.

Philip had contracted a marriage, after Mary's death, with the daughter of that terrible woman Catherine de Medici, widow of Henry II. of France, and there is every reason to believe that it was this Duke of Alva who planned the Massacre of St. Bartholomew. There were sinister conferences between Catherine, Philip, and Alva, and little doubt exists that the hideous tragedy which occurred in Paris on the night of August 24,

1572, was arranged in Madrid, and had its first inception in the cruel breast of Alva.

There had not been much love existing before between Philip and Elizabeth, who it is said had refused the hand of her Spanish brother-in-law. But after her interference in the Netherlands, and when her ships were intercepting and waylaying Spanish ships returning with treasure from the West, and when at last the one was the accepted champion of the Protestant, and the other of the Catholic cause, they became avowed enemies. Philip resolved to prepare a mighty armament for the invasion of England.

In 1587 Elizabeth sent Sir Francis Drake to reconnoiter and find out what Philip was doing. He appeared with twenty-five vessels before Cadiz. Having learned all he wanted, and burned a fleet of merchant vessels, he returned to his Queen.

In May, 1588, a fleet of one hundred and thirty ships, some "the largest that ever plowed the deep," sailed from Lisbon for the English coast. We may form some idea to-day of what must have been the feeling in England when this Armada, unparalleled in size, appeared in the English Channel. If

Sir Francis Drake's ships were fewer and smaller, he could match the Spaniards in audacity. He sent eight fireships right in among the close-lying vessels. Then, in the confusion which followed, while they were obstructed and entangled with their own fleet, he swiftly attacked them with such vigor that ten ships were sunk or disabled, and the entire fleet was demoralized. Then a storm overtook the fleeing vessels, and the winds and the waves completed the victory. As in the Spanish report of the disaster thirty-five is the number of ships acknowledged to be lost, we may imagine how great was the destruction. So ended Philip's invasion of England, and the great Spanish " Armada."

Philip II. died, 1598, in the Palace of the Escurial which he had built, and with that event ends the story of Spain's greatness. The period of one hundred and twenty-five years, including the reigns of Ferdinand and Isabella, of Charles V., and of Philip II., is, in a way, one of unmatched splendor. Spain had not like England by slow degrees expanded into great proportions, but through strange and perfectly fortuitous circumstances, she had, from a proud obscurity, suddenly leaped into a position of commanding power and magnificence. Fortune threw into her lap the greatest prize she ever had to bestow, and at the same time gave her two sovereigns of exceptional qualities and abilities. The story of this double reign is the romance, the fairy tale of history. Then came the magnificent reign of Charles V. with more gifts from fortune—the imperial crown, if not a substantial benefit to Spain, still bringing dignity and éclat. But under this glittering surface there had commenced even then a decline. Under Philip II. she was still magnificent, Europe was bowing down to her, but the decline was growing more manifest; and with the accession of his puny son, Philip III., there was little left but a brilliant past, which a proud and retrospective nation was going to feed upon for over three centuries. But it takes some time for such dazzling effulgence to disappear. The glamour of the Spanish name was going to last a long time and picturesquely veil her decay. The memory of such an ascendancy in Europe nourished the intense national pride of her people. The name Castilian took on a new significance.

Nor can we wonder at their pride in the

name "Castilian." Its glory was not the capricious gift of fortune, but won by a devotion, a constancy, and a fidelity of purpose which are unique in the history of the world. For seven hundred years the race for which that name stands had kept alive the national spirit, while their land was occupied by an alien civilization. These were centuries of privation and suffering and hardship; but never wavering in their purpose, and by brave deeds which have filled volumes, they reclaimed their land and drove out the Moors.

This is what gives to the name " Castilian," its proud significance. But when degenerate Hidalgos and Grandees, debauched by wealth and luxury, gloried in the name; when by rapacity and cruelty they destroyed the lands their valor had won; and when the Inquisition became their pastime and the rack and the wheel their toys—then the name Castilian began to take on a sinister meaning. Spain's most glorious period was not when she was converting the Indies and Mexico and Peru into a hell, not when Charles V. was playing his great game of diplomacy in Europe, but in that pre-Columbian era when a brave and rugged people were keeping alive their national life in the mountains of the Asturias. Well may Spain do honor to that time by calling the heir to her throne the " Prince of the Asturias!"

CHAPTER XIX.

THE history of the century after the death of Philip II. is one of rapid decline; with no longer a powerful master-mind to hold the state together. Every year saw the court at Madrid more splendid, and the people,—that insignificant factor,—more wretched, and sinking deeper and deeper into poverty. In fact, in spite of the fabulous wealth which fortune had poured upon her, Spain was becoming poor. But nowhere in Europe was royalty invested with such dignity and splendor of ceremonial, and the ambitious Marie de Medici, widow of Henry IV., was glad to form alliances for her children with those of Philip III. The "Prince of the Asturias," who was soon to become Philip IV., married her daughter, Isabella de Bourbon, and the Infanta, his sister, was at the same time married to the young Louis XIII., King of France.

The remnant of the Moors who still

lingered in the land were called *Moriscos;* and under a very thin surface of submission to Christian Spain, they nursed bitter memories and even hopes that some miracle would some day restore them to what was really the land of their fathers. A very severe edict, promulgated by Philip II., compelling conformity in all respects with Christian living, and—as if that were not a part of Christian living—forbidding *ablutions,* led to a serious revolt. And this again led to the forcible expulsion of every Morisco in Spain.

In 1609, by order of Philip III., the last of the Moors were conveyed in galleys to the African coast whence they had come just nine hundred years before.

In a narrative so drenched with tears, it is pleasant to hear of light-hearted laughter. We are told that when the young King Philip III. saw from his window a man striking his forehead and laughing immoderately he said: " That man is either mad, or he is reading ' Don Quixote ' "—which latter was the case. But the story written by Cervantes did more than entertain. Chivalry had lingered in the congenial soil of Spain long after it had disappeared in every other part of Europe; but when in the person of Don Quixote it was made to appear so utterly ridiculous, it was heard of no more.

Philip III., who died in 1621, was succeeded by his son Philip IV. As in the reign of his father worthless favorites ruled, while a profligate king squandered the money of the people in lavish entertainments and luxuries. Much has been written about the visit of Charles, Prince of Wales (afterward Charles I.), accompanied by the Duke of Buckingham, at his court; whither the young Prince had come disguised, to see the Infanta, Philip's sister, whom he thought of making his queen. Probably she did not please him, or perhaps the alliance with Protestant England was not acceptable to the pious Catholic family of Philip. At all events, Henrietta, sister of Louis XIII. of France, was his final choice, and shared his terrible misfortunes a few years later.

A revolt of the Catalonians on the French frontier led to a difficulty with France, which was finally adjusted by the celebrated "treaty of the Pyrenees." In this treaty was included the marriage of the young King Louis XIV. and Maria Theresa, daughter of Philip IV., the King of Spain. The European Powers would only consent to this union upon condition that Louis should solemnly renounce all claim to the Spanish crown for himself and his heirs; which promise had later a somewhat eventful history.

Seven of the United Provinces had achieved their independence during the reign of the third Philip, who had also driven out of his kingdom six hundred thousand Moriscos; by far the most skilled and industrious portion of the community. And now, at the close of the reign of Philip IV., the kingdom was further dimnished by the loss of Portugal; which, in 1664, the Lusitanians recovered, and proclaimed the Duke of Braganza King. When we add to this the loss of much of the Netherlands, and of the island of Jamaica, and concessions here and there to France and to Italy, it will be obvious that a process of contraction had soon followed that of Spain's phenomenal expansion!

During the reign of Charles II., who succeeded his father (1665), Spain was still further diminished by the cession to Louis XIV., in 1678, of more provinces in the Low Countries, which included the region now known as Alsace and Lorraine; which, it will be remembered, have in our own time passed from the keeping of France to that of victorious Germany.

There is one more incident in this reign which deserves at this time a passing notice. It was between the years 1670 and 1686 that the Spaniard and the Anglo-Saxon had their first collision in America. St. Augustine had been founded in 1565, and the old Spanish colony was much disturbed in 1663, when Charles II. of England planted an English colony in their near neighborhood (the Carolinas). During a war between Spain and England at the time above mentioned, feeling ran high between Florida and the Carolinas, and houses were burned and blood was shed. Spain had felt no concern about the little English colony planted on the bleak New England coast in 1620. Death by exposure and starvation promised speedily to remove that. But the settlement on the Carolinas was more serious, and at the same time the French were planting a colony of their own at the mouth of the Mississippi. The "lords of America" began to feel anxious about their control of the Gulf of Mexico. The cloud was a very small one, but it was not to be the last which would dim their skies in the West.

The one thing which gives historic importance to the reign of Carlos II. is that it marks the close—the ignominious close—of the great Hapsburg dynasty in Spain. And if the death of Carlos, in 1700, was a melancholy event, it is because with it the scepter so magnificently wielded by Ferdinand and Isabella passed to the keeping of the House of Bourbon, whose Spanish descendants have ruled Spain ever since.

CHAPTER XX.

THE last century had wrought great changes in European conditions. "The Holy Roman Empire," after a thirty-years' war with Protestantism, was shattered, and the Emperor of Germany was no longer the head of Europe. Protestant England had sternly executed Charles I., and then in the person of James II. had swept the last of the Catholic House of Stuart out of her kingdom. France, on the foundation laid by Richelieu, had developed into a powerful despotism, which her King, Louis XIV., was making magnificent at home and feared abroad.

For Spain it had been a century of steady decline, with loss of territory, power, and prestige. No longer great in herself, she was regarded by her ambitious neighbor, Louis XIV., as only a make-weight in the supremacy in Europe upon which he was determined. He had been ravaging the enfeebled German Empire, and now a friendly fate opened a peaceful door through which he might make Spain contribute to his greatness.

Carlos II. died (1700) without an heir. There was a vacant throne in Spain to which —on account of Louis' marriage, years before, with the Spanish Princess Maria Theresa— his grandson Philip had now the most valid claim. The other claimant, Archduke Karl, son of Leopold, Emperor of Germany, in addition to having a less direct hereditary descent, was unacceptable to the Spanish people, who had no desire to be ruled again by an occupant of the Imperial throne of Germany.

So, as Louis wished it, and the Spanish people also wished it, there was only one obstacle to his design; that was a promise made at the time of his marriage that he would never claim that throne for himself or his heirs. But when the Pope, after " prayerful deliberation," absolved him from that promise the way was clear. This grandson, just seventeen years old, was proclaimed Philip V., King of Spain, and Louis in the fullness of his heart exclaimed, " The Pyrenees have ceased to exist! "

Perhaps it would have been better for the

King if he had not made that dramatic exclamation. A man who could remove mountains to make a path for his ambitions might also drain seas! England took warning. She had been quietly bearing his insults for a long time, and not till he had impertinently threatened to place upon her throne the Pretender, an illegitimate son of James II., had she joined the coalition against the French King. But now she sent more armies, and a great captain to re-enforce Prince Eugene, who was fighting this battle for the Archduke Karl and for Europe.

But Louis had reached the summit. He was to go no higher than he had climbed when he uttered that vain boast. Philip V. was acknowledged King in 1702, and in 1704 *Blenheim* had been fought and won by Marlborough, and the decline of the *Grand Monarque* had commenced.

The war against him by a combined Europe now became the war of the "Spanish Succession." England and Holland united with Emperor Leopold to curb his limitless ambition. The purpose of the war of the "Spanish Succession" was, ostensibly, to place the Austrian Archduke upon the throne of Spain;

its real purpose was to check the alarming ascendancy of Louis XIV. in Europe.

It lasted for years, the poor young King and Queen being driven from one city to another, while the Austrian Archduke was at Madrid striving to reign over a people who would not recognize him.

Spain was being made the sport of three nations in pursuance of their own ambitious ends. Her land was being ravaged by foreign armies, recruited from three of her own disaffected provinces; while a young King with whom she was well satisfied was peremptorily ordered to make way for one Austria, England, and Holland preferred. It was a humiliating proof of the decline in national spirit, and the old Castilian pride must have sorely degenerated for such things to be possible.

Finally, after Louis XIV. had once more given solemn oath that the crowns of France and Spain should never be united, the "Peace of Utrecht" was signed (1713). But the provisions of the treaty were momentous for Spain. She was at one stroke of the pen stripped of half her possessions in Europe. Philip V. was acknowledged King of Spain and the Indies. But Sicily, with its regal title, was ceded to the Duke of Savoy; Milan, Naples, Sardinia, and the Netherlands went to Karl, now Emperor Charles VI. of Germany; while Minorca and Gibraltar passed to the keeping of England.

No one felt unmixed satisfaction, except perhaps England. The Archduke had failed to get his throne, and to wear the double crown like Charles V. Louis had carried his point. He had succeeded in keeping the kingdom for his grandson. But that kingdom was dismembered, and had shrunk to insignificant proportions in Europe, while England, most fortunate of all, had carried off the key to the Mediterranean. That little rocky promontory of Gibraltar was potentially of more value than all the rest!

Such was the beginning of the dynasty of the Bourbon in Spain. Philip was succeeded, upon his death in 1746, by his son Ferdinand VI., who also died, in 1759, and was succeeded by his brother, Philip's second son, who was known as Carlos III. When we try to praise these princes of the wretched Bourbon line, it is by mention of the evil they have refrained from doing rather than the good they have done. So Carlos III. is said to have done less harm to Spain than his predecessors. He established libraries and academies of science and of arts, and ruled like a kind-hearted gentleman, without the vices of his recent predecessors. His severity toward the Jesuits and their forcible expulsion from Spain, in 1767, are said to have been caused by personal resentment on account of some slanderous rumors regarding his birth, which were traced to them.

CHAPTER XXI.

But the fate of Spain was not now in the hands of her Kings. Be they good or evil she was destined henceforth to drift in the currents of *circumstance*, that sternest of masters, to whom her Kings as well as her people would be obliged helplessly to bow. All that she now possessed outside the borders of her own kingdom was the West Indies, her colonies in America, North and South, and the Philippines, that archipelago of a thousand isles in the southern Pacific, where Magellan was slain by the savage inhabitants after he had discovered it (1520).

Mexico and Peru had proved to be inexhaustible sources of wealth, and when the gold and silver diminished, the Viceroys in these and the other colonies could compel the people to wring rich products out of the soil, enough to supply Spain's necessities. The inhabitants of these colonies, who were Spanish with a slight admixture of the aboriginal races, had been treated as slaves and drudges for so many centuries that they never dreamed of resistance, nor questioned the justice of a fate which condemned them always to toil for Spain.

In the North the feeble colony planted in 1620 had expanded into thirteen vigorous English colonies. France, too, had been colonizing in America, and had drawn her frontier line from the mouth of the Mississippi to Canada. In 1755 a collision occurred between England and France over their American boundaries. By the year 1759, France had lost Quebec and every one of her strongholds, and she formed an alliance with Spain in a last effort to save her vanishing possessions in America.

Spain's punishment for this interference was swift. England dispatched ships, and promptly captured several West India islands, and the city of Havana, on this side of the globe; and Manila on the other. When we read of the Anglo-Saxon capturing Manila, and bombarding and capturing the city of Havana in the midsummer of 1762, we realize that history does sometimes repeat itself! And an interesting side-light is thrown upon "jingoism." We learn that when this war upon Spanish territory was contemplated, the boys in London were singing:

" We don't want to fight, but by Jingo if we do,
 We've got the ships, we've got the men, and we've got the money, too ! "

In the treaty which followed these victories, upon condition of England's returning Havana, and all the conquered territory excepting a portion of the West India Islands, Spain ceded to her the peninsula of Florida; while France, who was obliged to give to England all her territory east of the Mississippi, gave to Spain in return for her services the city of New Orleans, and all her territory west of the great river. This territory was retroceded to France by Spain in the year 1800, by the " Treaty of Madrid," and in 1803 was purchased by America from Napoleon, under the title of " Louisiana."

There was a growing irritation in the Spanish heart against England. She was crowding Spain out of North America, had insinuated herself into the West India Islands, and she was mistress of Gibraltar. So it was with no little satisfaction that they saw her involved in a serious quarrel with her American colonies, at a time when a stubborn and incompetent Hanoverian King was doing his best to destroy her. The hour seemed auspicious for recovering Gibraltar, and also to drive England out of the West Indies. The alliance with France had become a permanent one, and was known as a *family compact* between the Bourbon cousins Louis XV. and Carlos III. France had at this time rather distracting conditions at home; but she was thirsting for revenge at the loss of her rich American possessions, and besides, a sentimental interest in the brave people who had proclaimed their independence from the mother country, and were fighting to maintain it, began to manifest itself. It was fanned, no doubt, by a desire for England's humiliation; but it assumed a form too chivalric and too generous for Americans ever to discredit by unfriendly analysis of motive. Spain cared little for the cause of the colonies; but she was quite willing to help them by worrying and diverting the energies of England. So she invested Gibraltar. A garrison of only a handful of men astonished Europe by the bravery of its defense. Gibraltar was not taken by the Bourbon allies, neither were the English driven out of the West Indies. But it was a satisfaction to Spain to see her humbled by her victorious colonies!

So Carlos III. had indirectly assisted in the establishment of a republic on the confines of his Mexican Empire; apparently unconscious of the contagion in the word *independence*. But he quickly learned this to his sorrow. The story of the revolted and freed colonies sped on the wings of the wind. And in Peru a brave descendant of the Incas arose as a Deliverer. He led sixty thousand men into a vain fight for liberty. Of course the effort failed, but a spirit had been awakened which might be smothered, but never extinguished.

Carlos III. died in 1788 and was succeeded by his son Carlos IV.

During the miserable reign of this miserable King, France caught the infection from the free institutions in America. The Republic she had helped to create was fatal to monarchy in her own land. A revolution accompanied by unparalleled horrors swept away the whole tyrannous system of centuries and left the country a trembling wreck—but free. The dream of a republic was brief. Napoleon gathered the imperfectly organized government into his own hands, then by successive and rapid steps arose to Imperial power. France was an Empire, and adoringly submitted to the man who swiftly made her great and feared in Europe. She had another Charlemagne, who was bringing to his feet Kings and Princes, and annexing half of Europe to his empire!

It was an easy matter for this man to sweep away the poor, helpless Spanish Bourbon King, Carlos IV., and place on the throne of Spain his brother Joseph. So swiftly was it done, that Spain made no resistance, and she found herself fighting side by side with Napoleon in his battles for universal dominion. Perhaps she thought this invincible man might help her to get back Gibraltar and to drive the English out of the West Indies.

Napoleon hated England no less heartily than Spain, and in 1804, the French and Spanish fleets started out in pursuit of the English fleet under Nelson. For two years the two squadrons sailed back and forth from the Spanish coast to the West Indies, but failed to find each other. But at last, at Trafalgar, the long-expected meeting came. Nelson, on his flagship *Victory*, led twenty-seven ships of the line and four frigates. The allied fleet had thirty-four ships and seven frigates. The victory of the English was complete, but it cost them their great Admiral. Nelson was struck by a ball and died on the deck of his ship.

Gibraltar was not taken, the English were not defeated, and the Spanish people began to realize the humiliation they were under in the usurpation of the Spanish crown by Joseph Bonaparte, only recently an obscure Frenchman; a man destitute of ability, and only the obedient servant of the French Emperor.

But they had embarked in this Napoleonic campaign, and they must go on. And so, when Arthur Wellesley (Lord Wellington) came with a great army, battle after battle was fought, success leaning more and more to the English side, until a final rout of the allied armies proved the death knell of the reign of Joseph, who, it is said, ignominiously fled from the kingdom with one gold-piece in his pocket.

CHAPTER XXII.

THE decade between 1804 and 1814 was very barren in external benefits to Spain, with her King held in "honorable captivity" in France, and the obscure Joseph abjectly striving to please not his subjects, but his august brother Napoleon. But in the brief period after Joseph's flight, when there was no King, no despotic government to stifle popular sentiment, the unsuspected fact developed that Spain had caught the infection of freedom!

In the absence of a King, the government devolved upon the Cortes. In 1812, this body drew up a new Constitution for Spain. So completely did this remodel the whole administration that the most despotic monarchy in Europe was transformed into the one most severely limited.

Great was the surprise of Ferdinand VI. when, in 1814, he came to the throne of his ejected father Carlos III., to find himself called upon to reign under a Constitution which made Spain almost as free as a republic. He promulgated a decree declaring the Cortes illegal and rescinding all its acts, the Constitution of 1812 included. Then when he had re-established the Inquisition, which had been abolished by the Cortes, when he had publicly burned the impertinent Constitution, and quenched conspiracies here and there, he settled himself for a comfortable reign after the good old arbitrary fashion.

The Napoleonic empire having been effaced by a combined Europe, Ferdinand's Bourbon cousins were in the same way restoring the excellent methods of their fathers in France.

But there was a spirit in the air which was not favorable to the peace of Kings. On the American coast there stood "Liberty Enlightening the World!" A growing, prosperous republic was a shining example of what might be done by a brave resistance to oppression and a determined spirit of independence.

The pestilential leaven of freedom had been at work while monarchies slept in security. Ferdinand discovered that not only was there a seditious sentiment in his own kingdom, but every one of his American colonies was in open rebellion, and some were even daring to set up free governments in imitation of the United States.

Not only was Ferdinand's sovereignty threatened, but the very principle of monarchy itself was endangered.

Russia, Austria, and Prussia formed themselves into a league for the preservation of what they were pleased to call " The Divine Right of Kings." It was the attack upon this sacred principle, which was the germ of all this mischievous talk about freedom. They called their league " The Holy Alliance," and what they proposed to do was to *stamp out free institutions in the germ.*

In pursuance of this purpose, in 1819 there appeared at Cadiz a large fleet, assembled for the subjugation of Spanish America.

But there was an Anglo-Saxon America, which had a preponderating influence in that land now; and there was also an Anglo-Saxon race in Europe which had its own views about the " Divine Right of Kings," and also concerning the mission of the " Holy Alliance."

The right of three European Powers to restore to Spain her revolted colonies in America was denied by President Monroe; not upon the ground of Spain's inhumanity, and the inherent right of the colonies to an independence which they might achieve. Such was the nature of England's protest, through her Minister Canning. But President Monroe's contention rested on a much broader ground. In a message delivered in 1823 he uttered these words: " European Powers must not extend their political systems to any portion of the American continent." The meaning of this was that *America has been won for freedom;* and no European Power will be permitted to establish a monarchy, nor to coerce in any way, nor to suppress inclinations toward freedom, in any part of the Western Hemisphere. This is the " Monroe Doctrine "; a doctrine which, although so startling in 1832, had in 1896 become so firmly imbedded in the minds of the people, that Congress decided it to be a vital principle of American policy.

But there was another and more serious obstacle in the way of the proposed plan for subjugating the Spanish-American colonies. The army assembled by the Holy Alliance at Cadiz was an offense to the people who had seen their Constitution burned and their hopes of a freer government destroyed. Officers and troops refused to embark, and joined a concourse of disaffected people at Cadiz. A smothered popular sentiment burst forth into a series of insurrections throughout Spain, and the astonished Ferdinand was compelled, in 1820, to acknowledge the Constitution of 1812. This was not upholding the principle of the "Divine Right of Kings"! So, under the direction of the Holy Alliance, a French army of one hundred thousand men moved into Spain, took possession of her capital, and for two years administered her affairs under a regency, and then reinstated Ferdinand, leaving a French army of occupation.

In this contest two distinct political parties had developed—the Liberal party and the party of Absolutism. As Ferdinand VI. became the choice of the Liberals, and his brother Don Carlos of the party of Absolutism, we must infer either that it was a Liberalism of a very mild type, or that Ferdinand's views had been modified since the "Holy Alliance" took his kingdom into its own keeping. But his brother Carlos was the adored of the Absolutists, and a plot was made to compel Ferdinand to abdicate in his favor. This was the first of the Carlist plots, which, with little intermission, and always in the interest of despotism and bigotry, have menaced the safety and well-being of Spain ever since. From the year 1825 to 1898 there has been always a Don Carlos to trouble the political waters in that land.

So the mission of the " Holy Alliance " had failed. Instead of rehabilitating the sacred principle of the " Divine Right of Kings," they saw a powerful liberal party established in a kingdom which was the very stronghold of despotism. And instead of stamping out free institutions, six Spanish-American colonies had been recognized as free and independent states (1826). Spain had for three centuries ruled the richest and the fairest land on the earth. She had shown herself utterly undeserving of the opportunity, and unfit for the responsibilities imposed by a great colonial empire. She had sown the wind and now she reaped the whirlwind. She did not own a foot of territory on the continent she had discovered!

CHAPTER XXIII.

IN 1833 King Ferdinand VI. died, leaving one child, the Princess Isabella, who was three years old. Here was the opportunity for the adherents of Don Carlos.

The "Salic law" had been one of the Gothic traditions of ancient Spain, and had with few exceptions been in force until 1789; when Charles IV. issued a "Pragmatic Sanction," establishing the succession through the female as well as the male line; and on April 6, 1830, King Ferdinand confirmed this decree; so, when Isabella was born, October 10, 1830, she was heiress to the throne, *unless* her ambitious uncle, Don Carlos, could set aside the decree abrogating the old Salic law, and reign as Carlos IV.

In the three years before his brother's death he had laid his plans for the coming crisis. Isabella was proclaimed Queen under the regency of her depraved mother Christina. The extreme of the Catholic party, and of the reactionary or absolutist party, flocked about the Carlist standard; while the party of the infant Queen was the rallying point for the liberal and progressive sentiment in the kingdom; and her cause had the support of the new reform government of Louis Philippe in France, and of lovers of freedom elsewhere.

The party of the Queen triumphed. But the Carlists survived; and, like the Bourbons in France, have ever since in times of political peril been a serious element to be reckoned with.

During the infancy of the Queen, Spain was the prey of unceasing party dissensions; Don Carlos again and again trying to overthrow her government, and again and again being driven a fugitive over the Pyrenees; while the Queen Regent, who was secretly married to her Chamberlain, the son of a tobacconist in Madrid, was bringing disgrace and odium upon the Liberal party which she was supposed to lead.

In 1843 the Cortes declared that the Queen had attained her majority. Her disgraced mother was driven out of the country and Isabella II. ascended her throne. Isabella had a younger sister, Maria Louisa, and in 1846 the double marriage of these two children was celebrated with great splendor at Madrid. The Queen was married to her cousin Don Francisco d'Assisi, and her sister to the Duke de Montpensier, fifth son of Louis Philippe.

If, upon the birth of Liberalism in Spain, that kingdom could have been governed by a wise and competent sovereign, the concluding chapters of this narrative might have been very different. No time could have been less favorable for a radical change in policy than the period during which Isabella II. was Queen of Spain. Personally she was all that a woman and a Queen should not be. With apparently not an exalted desire or ambition for her country, this depraved daughter of a depraved mother pursued her downward course until 1868, when the nation would bear no more. A revolution broke out. Isabella, with her three children, fled to France and there was once more a vacant throne in Spain.

The hopes of the Carlists ran high. But the Cortes came to an unexpected decision. They would have no Spanish Bourbon, be he Carlist or Liberal. The reigning dynasty in Italy was at this moment the adored of the Liberals in Europe. So they offered the Crown to Amadeo, second son of Humbert,

King of Italy (1870). Three years were quite sufficient for this experiment. The young Amadeo was as glad to take off his crown and to leave his kingdom, as the people were to have him do so. He abdicated in 1873.

The Liberal party had been regretting their loss of opportunity in 1870. France had passed through many political phases in the last few years, and the present French Republic had just come into existence. Again Spain caught the contagion from her neighbor, and Spanish Liberalism became *Republicanism*.

When Castelar, that patriotic and sagacious statesman, friend of Garibaldi, of Mazzini, and of Kossuth, led this movement, many hopefully believed the political millennium was at hand, when Spain was about to join the brotherhool of Republics! But something more than a great leader is needed to create a Republic. The magic of Castelar's eloquence, the purity of his character, and the force of his convictions were powerless to hold in stable union the conflicting elements with which he had to deal. The Carlists were scheming, and the Cortes was driven to an immediate decision.

The fugitive Queen Isabella had with her in exile a young son Alfonso, seventeen years of age. Alfonso was invited to return upon the sole condition that his mother should be excluded from his kingdom. An insurrection which was being fomented by Don Carlos II. led to this action of the Cortes, which was perhaps the wisest possible under the circumstances. The young Prince of the legitimate Bourbon line was proclaimed King Alfonso XII. in 1874.

A romantic marriage with his cousin Mercedes, daughter of the Duke de Montpensier, to whom he was deeply attached, speedily took place. Only five months later Mercedes died and was laid in the gloomy Escurial. A marriage was then arranged with Christina, an Austrian Archduchess, who was brought to Madrid, and there was another marriage celebrated with much splendor. The infant daughter, who was born a few years later, was named Mercedes; a loving tribute to the adored young Queen he had lost, which did credit as much to Christina as to Alfonso.

The hard school of exile had, no doubt, been an advantage to Alfonso; and at the outset of his reign he won the confidence of the

Liberals by saying "he wished them to understand he was the first Republican in Europe; and when they were tired of him they had only to tell him so, and he would leave as quickly as Amadeo had done." There was not time to test the sincerity of these assurances. Alfonso XII. died in 1885, and joined Mercedes and his long line of predecessors in the Escurial. Five months later his son was born, and the throne which had been filled by the little Mercedes passed to the boy who was proclaimed Alfonso XIII. of Spain, under the Regency of his mother Queen Christina.

CHAPTER XXIV.

At the beginning of the nineteenth century the foreign dominions of Spain, although reduced, were still a vast and imperial possession. The colonial territory over which Alfonso XIII. was to have sovereignty at the close of that century, consisted of the Philippines, the richest of the East Indies; Cuba, the richest of the West Indies; Porto Rico, and a few outlying groups of islands of no great value.

Nowhere had the Constitution of 1812 awakened more hope than in Cuba; and from the setting aside of that instrument by Ferdinand VI. dates the existence of an insurgent party in that beautiful but most unhappy island. Ages of spoliation and cruelty and wrong had done their work. The iron of oppression had entered into the soul of the Cuban. There was a deep exasperation which refused to be calmed. From thenceforth annexation to the United States, or else a "*Cuba Libre*," was the determined, and even desperate aim.

After a ten-years' war, 1868-78, the people yielded to what proved a delusive promise of home-rule. How could Spain bestow upon her colony what she did not possess herself? When in 1881 she tried to pacify Cuba by permitting that island to send six Senators to sit in the Spanish Cortes, it was a phantom of a phantom. There was no outlet for the national will in Spain itself. Her Cortes was *not* a national assembly, and its members were *not* the choice of the people. How much less must they be so then in Cuba, where they were only men of straw selected by the home government, for the purpose of defeating— not expressing—the popular will? The emptiness of this gift was soon discovered. Then came a shorter conflict, which was only a prelude to the last.

A handful of ragged revolutionists, ignorant of the arts of war, commenced the final struggle for liberty on February 24, 1895, under the leadership of José Marti. At the end of two years a poorly armed band of guerrilla soldiers had waged a successful contest against 235,000 well-equipped troops, supported by a militia and a navy, and maintained by supplies from Spain; had adopted a Constitution, and were asking for recognition as a free Republic. The Spanish commander Martinez Campos was superseded by General Weyler (1895), and a new and severer method was inaugurated in dealing with the stubborn revolutionists, but with no better success than before. In August, 1897, an insurrection broke out in the Philippines, and Spain was in despair.

America calmly resisted all appeals for annexation or for intervention in Cuba. Sympathy for Cuban patriots was strong in the hearts of the people, but the American Government steadfastly maintained an attitude of strict neutrality and impartiality, and with unexampled patience saw a commerce amounting annually to one hundred millions of dollars wiped out of existence, her citizens reduced to want by the destruction of their property,— some of them lying in Spanish dungeons subjected to barbarities which were worthy of the Turkish Janizaries; our fleets used as a coastguard and a police, in the protection of Spanish interests, and more intolerable than all else, our hearts wrung by cries of anguish at our very doors!

But when General Weyler inaugurated a

system for the deliberate starvation of thirty thousand "Reconcentrados," an innocent peasantry driven from their homes and herded in cities, there to perish, the limit of patience was reached. It was this touch of human pity—this last and intolerable strain upon our sympathies—which turned the scale.

While a profound feeling of indignation was prevailing on account of these revolting crimes against humanity, the battleship *Maine* was, by request of Consul General Lee at that place, dispatched to the harbor of Havana to guard American citizens and interests. The sullen reception of the *Maine* was followed on February 15, 1898, by a tragedy which shocked the world. Whether the destruction of that ship and the death of 266 brave men was from internal or external causes was a very critical question. It was submitted to a court of inquiry which, after long deliberation, rendered the decision that the cause was —*external*.

It looked dark for lovers of peace! President McKinley exhausted all the resources of diplomacy before he abandoned hope of a peaceful adjustment which would at the same time compel justice to the Cuban people.

But on April 25, 1898, it was declared that war existed between Spain and America.

On May 1 Commodore Dewey achieved a victory over the Spanish fleet at Manila unmatched in the history of naval warfare. With Admiral Dewey virtual master of the Philippines, and Admiral Sampson investing the island of Cuba, there seems little doubt that the colonial empire of Spain is at an end, and centuries of cruelty are avenged.

The ancient kingdom over which Alfonso XIII. expects to rule is tending to its fall. It requires small prophetic vision to see that Turkey in the east of Europe, and Spain in the west must soon give way to the advancing tide of modern civilization. A people whose national festival is a bull-fight, is as much of an anachronism in this closing century as is one whose most revered institution is a harem.

Cruelty is not in favor with the world today; and whether in Bulgaria, or Armenia, or in Havana, *it will not be borne.* A nation which converts the fairest island on earth into a human shambles has put herself beyond the pale of the family of other Christian nations.

Spain is mediæval in her methods and ideals. In the time of her opulence and splendor these methods and ideals were hers. So she believes in them and clings to them still. She is the victim of a vicious political system, to which an intensely proud, patriotic, and brave people believe they must be loyal.

In no other land—as we have seen—is the national spirit so strong. Certainly nowhere else has it ever been subjected to such strain and survived. And this intense loyalty, this overwhelming pride of race, this magnificent valor, are all summoned to uphold a poor, perishing, vicious political system, which has not one heart-beat in harmony with the world in which it lingers.

We believe there are warm and generous hearts, and men good and true in Spain to-day. Nowhere has liberal sentiment found a leader more exalted than is Castelar. So how paralyzing must be the existing political conditions, when a man such as he finds his path of duty in upholding such a government and such enormities!

For the redemption of Turkey there is no hope. That is a mass of corruption which vultures and natural processes will ere long remove. But for Spain—beautiful but erring Spain—there may still be a future.

"What doth the Lord require of thee but to do justly,—to love mercy,—and to walk humbly before thy god."

THE END.

LIST OF VISIGOTH KINGS.

	A. D.
Ataulfus,	411-415
Wallia,	415-420
Theodored,	420-451
Thorismund,	451-452
Theodoric I. (Defeated Attila),	452-466
Evaric (Completed Gothic Conquest in Spain),	466-483
Alaric,	483-506
Gesaleic,	506-511
Theodoric II.,	511-522
Amalaric,	522-531
Theudis,	531-548
Theudisel,	548-549
Agilan,	549-554
Athanagild I.,	554-567
Liuva I.,	567-570
Leovigild,	570-587
Recared I.,	587-601
Liuva II.,	601-603
Witteric,	603-610
Gundemar,	610-612
Sisebert,	612-621
Recared II. (3 months).	
Swintila,	621-631
Sisenand,	631-636
Chintila,	636-640
Tulga,	640-642

LIST OF VISIGOTH KINGS.

	A. D.
Chindaswind,	642–649
Receswind,	649–672
Wamba,	672–680
Ervigius,	680–687
Egica (son of Wamba),	687–701
Witiza,	701–709
Roderick,	709–711
Theodomir, } Kings without a kingdom {	711–743
Athanagild II.,	743–755

KINGS OF THE ASTURIAS AND LEON.

	A. D.
Pelayo (of Royal Gothic birth),	718
Favila (son of above),	737
Alfonso I. (son-in-law of Pelayo),	739
Fruela I. (son of Alfonso),	757
Aurelio,	768
Mauregato,	774
Bermudo I.,	788
Alfonso II.,	791
Ramiro I.,	842
Ordoño I.,	850
Alfonso III.,	866
Garcia,	910
Ordoño II.,	914
Fruela II.,	923
Alfonso IV.,	925
Ramiro II.,	930
Ordoño III.,	950
Sancho I.,	955
Ramiro III.,	967
Bermudo II.,	982
Alfonso V.,	999
Bermudo III.,	1027
Fernando I. (also King of Castile),	1037
Alfonso VI.,	1065
Urraca,	1109
Alfonso VII. (also King of Castile),	1126

KINGS OF THE ASTURIAS AND LEON.

	A. D.
Fernando II.,	1157
Alfonso IX. (Aided Conquest of Moors),	1188
Fernando III.,	1230

LEON AND CASTILE UNITED.

Alfonso X. (*el sabio*),	1252
Sancho IV.,	1284
Fernando IV.,	1295
Alfonso XI.,	1312
Pedro I. (*el cruel*),	1350
Enrique II.,	1369
Juan I.,	1379
Enrique IV.,	1454
Isabel I. (married to Fernando II. of Aragon),	1474

CASTILE AND ARAGON UNITED.

Carlos I. (Charles I. Elected Charles V. of Germany, 1519),	1516
Philip II.,	1556
Philip III.,	1593
Philip IV.,	1621
Carlos II.,	1665

HOUSE OF BOURBON.

Philip V.,	1700
Fernando VI.,	1746
Carlos III.,	1759
Ferdinand VII.,	1799
Joseph Bonaparte,	1806
Ferdinand VII. (reinstated),	1814
Isabella II. (She was dethroned, 1868),	1833
Alfonso XII.,	1874
Alfonso XIII.,	1885

BIBLIOGRAPHY FOR SPAIN.

1. Ginn's "Ancient Atlas."
2. Myers' "Ancient History."
3. Myers' "Mediæval History."
4. Gibbon's "Rome."
5. Morris' "The Beginnings of the Middle Ages."
6. Brinton's "Races and Peoples."
7. Johnson's "Cyclopedia."
8. "Encyclopædia Britannica."
9. Prescott's "Peru and Mexico."
10. Prescott and Robertson's "Charles V."
11. Prescott and Robertson's "Philip II."
12. Motley's "Dutch Republic."
13. Hale's "History of Spain."
14. Lane-Poole's "Moors in Spain."
15. Watt's "Recovery of Spain."
16. Irving's "Conquest of Granada."
17. Chart of Civilization, "Who, When, and What."
18. A History of Spain in less than 40 pages, by Mary Platt Parmele.

www.ingramcontent.com/pod-product-compliance
Lightning Source LLC
Chambersburg PA
CBHW032152160426
43197CB00008B/877